Pleas

Yo

You

_____
\

WILLIAM
TYNDALE

WILLIAM TYNDALE

A very brief history

MELVYN BRAGG

First published in Great Britain in 2017

Society for Promoting Christian Knowledge
36 Causton Street
London SW1P 4ST
www.spck.org.uk

British Library Cataloguing-in-Publication Data
A catalogue record for this book is available from the British Library

ISBN 978–0–281–07713–7
eBook ISBN 978–0–281–07715–1

1 3 5 7 9 10 8 6 4 2

Typeset by Manila Typesetting Company
Printed in Great Britain by TJ International

eBook by Manila Typesetting Company

Produced on paper from sustainable forests

To St Mary's Church, Wigton,
where I first encountered the words
of William Tyndale

Contents

Preface

Many of the contributors to this series are academics. I am not.

My interest in Tyndale followed a personal and winding road. I came across him, unconsciously of course, when I heard extracts from the King James Bible read out twice on Sundays in the Anglican church in which I was a choir-boy and five mornings a week in the assembly at the local grammar school. I did not realize how deeply Tyndale was implanted in the prose: phrases which remain with me in the last lap of my life.

I first understood his influence on the Authorized Version when I wrote a history of the English language called *The Adventure of English* (2003). I had turned to the King James Bible as a key part of the *Adventure* and it was here that I became fully aware of William Tyndale's contribution. I was amazed and intrigued by this and became and remain very affected by the man himself. In my view he has claim to be one of the very greatest Englishmen.

This admiration continued into another book of mine called *Twelve Books That Changed the World* (2006) (I should have subtitled it, 'by British authors'). Again there was the King James Bible and again there was much Tyndale.

With Anna Cox, a prize-winning BBC producer, I made a film about Tyndale (2013). On transmission, despite Tyndale's general low profile in this country and the very modest pre-publicity, it was put out at a good time on a Thursday evening (9 p.m.) and to everyone's astonishment it got a bigger audience than BBC1 and it was a close-run thing with ITV. The appetite for Tyndale it seemed was out there.

My research, then, was done along the way. For those books and programmes, I am grateful to Dr John Guy of Cambridge University, mentioned in the text; and Nasim Tadghighi (University of Bristol), who spoke about 'practice of prelates' and the 'the obedience of a Christian man'. There are also a couple we filmed who did not make the final cut but were invaluable: Dr David Harry (Late Medieval historian and visiting lecturer at Chester University), who talked in great detail about Foxe, and Guido Latre, our guide for the film in Antwerp and a passionate disciple of Tyndale. Guido is the Professor of English Literature and Culture at the University of Louvain.

There were also contributions from Anna Cox herself and those she worked with in the BBC.

But my chief source and rock was David Daniell's *William Tyndale: A Biography* (1993). This is a quite magnificent work and I was greatly indebted to it throughout.

Inside the book I credit all the main sources as I go along, for example, Foxe's *Book of Martyrs*, or where not that work, his *Acts and Monuments*. The quotes from Tyndale himself are flagged as coming from either a prologue or a preface or one of his essays. Thomas Cromwell's letters and Stephen Vaughan's replies and reports are flagged, as are sources for conversations in the West Country in Tyndale's early years, especially those of Richard Webb of Chipping Sodbury.

I am also, as so often, grateful to my friend Julia Matheson for her invaluable support.

Chronology

1494	Born in Melksham Court, Stinchcombe, Gloucestershire. The family also went by the name Hychyns (Hitchins), and had moved from Northumberland in the fifteenth century. It was wealthy and well-connected.
1506	Went to Magdalen College School. From there he moved to Magdalen College, Oxford University, to begin a Bachelor of Arts degree.
1512	Received his BA. Became a sub-deacon.
1515	Made a Master of Arts. This allowed him to start to study theology. He showed an exceptional talent as a linguist.
1517–21	Went to Cambridge. Erasmus had studied there and, although he had left in 1512, his influence, particularly his Greek New Testament (1515), was strong. In 1517 Luther's theses of condemnation of the Roman Catholic Church put Europe in an uproar. In 1521 Wolsey burned Luther's works in London.
1521	Tyndale became chaplain at the house of Sir John Walsh at Little Sodbury and tutor to his children. He pursued his study of Greek and may have begun translating the New Testament into English. He preached in public. His opinions were controversial.
1522	Summoned before John Ball, Chancellor of the Diocese of Worcester, for alleged heretical

opinions. The accusation was dropped after a dramatic and demeaning trial.

1523 Tyndale moved to London to look for work and the conditions in which he could translate the Bible into English. The Bishop of London, Cuthbert Tunstall, offered him no encouragement, and after a year in London, with the help of a family connection in the wool trade, and during which time he lectured and worked alone, he realized there would be no work for him in London.

1524 Tyndale left London for 'Europe', possibly going to Wittenberg.

1525 Completed his translation of the New Testament. Its publication by Peter Quentell in Cologne was interrupted by men in the pay of Henry VIII's court.

1526 Tyndale fled to Worms, and his New Testament was published by Peter Schoeffer. It was smuggled into England and Scotland amid growing anti-Lutheranism. Tyndale was seen as a dangerous Lutheran. Copies of the book were burned in public by Bishop Tunstall, and Cardinal Wolsey condemned Tyndale as a heretic.

1527 Published *The Parable of the Wicked Mammon*, which further inflamed the English establishment.

1528 Published *The Obedience of a Christian Man*, which was much appreciated by Henry VIII, introduced to it by Anne Boleyn.

1530	Published *The Practice of Prelates*, which opposed Henry VIII's planned annulment of his marriage to Katherine of Aragon. Henry asked Emperor Charles V to have Tyndale arrested and returned to England. Studied Hebrew.
1530–34	Thomas Cromwell made attempts to persuade Tyndale to return. Tyndale involved in a lengthy and incendiary quarrel and correspondence with Sir Thomas More. Living in Antwerp, working on the Old Testament, learning Hebrew, revising the New Testament, which was published in 1534.
1535	Tyndale was seized by the imperial authorities in Antwerp, having been betrayed by Henry Phillips, and imprisoned in Vilvoorde Castle near Brussels.
1535	'Coverdale's Bible' (in English) was published in London, the first of many Tyndale-dependent versions which peaked in the King James Bible in 1611. Over 90 per cent of the New Testament in that Bible was Tyndale's work, and more than 80 per cent in the books of the Old Testament translated by Tyndale.
1536	Tyndale was tried on a charge of heresy and condemned to death. On 6 October Tyndale was 'strangled to death while tied to the stake and his body was burned'. His last words were, 'Lord, open the King of England's eyes!'

Part 1

THE HISTORY

1

Innocence and genius

On the morning of 6 October 1536, a frail scholar was taken from a dungeon in the castle at Vilvoorde, just north of Brussels. Armed guards kept the crowds at bay as he was led through the streets of the small town. He was to be strangled, then burned. The funeral pyre, a wigwam stack of planks surmounted by a cross, was ready. Gunpowder would be thrown on the wood to encourage the flames. He was allowed a few moments of prayer. As a priest, prayer had been the keystone of his faith. After the brief pause, he walked up the steps to be tied to the cross. As he waited for the flames, he called out, 'Lord, open the King of England's eyes!'

This was William Tyndale, the man whose translation of the New Testament and much of the Old Testament was to bring about more profound changes to the English-speaking world over the next five centuries than the works of any other man in its history. He was noted for his genius as a translator, for his loyalty to the English King, Henry VIII, for the unblemished purity of his life and for his combination of innocence and fearlessness. For years he had been hunted down by spies from the court of Henry VIII, from the Vatican and from the court of the Holy Roman Emperor. Finally, with the betrayal of a Judas, he was captured, imprisoned, tormented and martyred.

His crime was his unbreakable determination throughout his life, whatever it cost, to give to the English people a

Bible in their own language. Against all but crushing odds, over a short adult lifetime spent in constant danger and deprivation and despite unspeakable sadistic cruelties by the English court and clergy, he succeeded.

The English language, largely based on his translation, subsequently swept around the globe. It liberated thought, seeded Protestantism and inspired books, pamphlets, art, songs, protests and poetry. There has never been anybody to match his achievement. The quiet English priest and scholar transformed the world of words. He gave his life so that ours could be lived in what he saw as the language of truth.

* * *

Like most of the greatest minds, William Tyndale set his life's purpose when he was a boy. It is as if these people of genius – Newton, Darwin, the Brontë sisters – somehow understand their life's work in childhood and, not wasting a minute, pursue it obsessively until death. When he was a boy, Tyndale read about the Saxon King of England, Athelstan, who had ordered parts of the Bible to be translated into the language of the proud English successors to Alfred the Great. In one of the few autobiographical notes that Tyndale left behind, he wrote of this in terms which transparently declare the origin of what would become a life bound to the renewal of that ancient English aim: English for the English.

William Tyndale of Gloucestershire, son of a family whose wealth was based on the flourishing English woollen trade, would succeed. He would rise out of the natural sculpture of the beautiful and comfortable Cotswold landscape and set out on a mission which would wholly possess his life.

His aim was to overthrow the language of power as well as its structure. This was one of the most effective forces of control in the world – the Holy Roman Catholic Church.

This structure of riches and vast influence claimed to be the sole guardian of the keys to eternal life and to the fate of the soul. It laid down the fundamental rules of behaviour and the truth of God's Word. This Word since 381 had been in Latin and, by the time of Tyndale's birth in 1494, this Latin version, called the Vulgate, encrusted in sanctity, was never to be challenged. Its meanings were the monopoly of the Pope in Rome.

In 1494, England looked as if it were settling down under the first Tudor, Henry VII, after decades of wars abroad and in England itself. Its rulers were still a privileged landowning warrior tribe largely descended from Normans since the Battle of Hastings. Its religious hierarchs were again mainly bred from Norman stock. Religion was the other side of the ruling coin. The King governed through his warriors with some influence from Parliament and the Law. From the Church, which was an arm of politics, he demanded and largely got obedience in return for allowing it exceptional privileges. And the Church controlled entry to heaven.

The monasteries and cathedrals of England were very grand. Their magnificence was never disputed. Nor was their usefulness – resting places for the poor, schools for some of the children and the biggest employer of men and women in the kingdom. Their patronage of builders, glaziers and skilled artisans was key to the economy. Rievaulx Abbey in Yorkshire, for instance, was a key supplier of wool to the 'European' market and, with its technological inventions, was well on the way to enhancing wool production radically. Above all, they were sites and silos of prayer.

Prayer was seen as the driving force of medieval life. God listened to Christians. He was available to the pure in heart. Prayers utterly dominated a monastic foundation – eight or more full services through the day and night. And the wealthy gave often spectacular sums of money, gifts of land and treasure, to these religious institutions in return for daily targeted prayers for the advance of their souls towards heaven. The unseen soul was the most vital organ in medieval Catholic life. The purpose of life was the salvation of one's soul at death. On this rock the authorities in Rome had over many years built a stupendous edifice – including the marketing of purgatory, penitence and pilgrimage – which raked in a fortune for the Church.

In the Cotswolds, as elsewhere, there were doubts and murmurings, and some there who welcomed the Lollards. The young Tyndale, sharp and acute as he seems to have been from boyhood, must have been aware of the comings and goings of these mysterious, prohibited, admired young men. The Lollards were disciples of John Wycliffe, an Oxford philosopher who in the 1380s had organized the translation of the Bible into English. This was in some ways – especially compared with Tyndale's – often a rather lumpen effort, but it was an enormous statement. At that time, to translate the Word of God into English was, in ecclesiastical terms, heresy – a crime against the faith and one which could lead to death. Wycliffe's Bible was banned in the 1380s.

But Wycliffe's legacy would not be erased. Throughout the fifteenth century and beyond, his followers – young, well-educated men, usually from Oxford – trod the lesser-used paths and tracks through the greenwoods, valleys and hills of England. They brought copies of this illegal book to those who, like them, wanted to read or hear the words of God and of Christ, the Gospels and the Prophets in their own tongue. It was perilous. If caught, these men were tortured for further information and often as not executed. Both Church and State combined to stamp out this heresy. There is still, today, a torture chamber in the London residence of the Archbishop of Canterbury known as the Lollards' Tower.

English was feared because the Bible had become a sacred token and taboo, an untouchable authority. It was in Latin. When Jerome translated the Bible at the end of the fourth century, Latin was generally spoken across the Roman Empire, which had by then adopted Christianity as its state religion. The translation was given the name 'Vulgate' because it was in the vulgar tongue – everyday Latin, not Aramaic (which the apostles spoke) or Greek (the first language of translation). Over the centuries native vernaculars had become increasingly capable of conveying all that was in the Vulgate but by then the Catholic Church's Bible had become their cornerstone. God spoke Latin. Churchmen knew Latin. Only churchmen and women could mediate directly with God.

Common sense and the Wycliffe Lollards questioned this. A small number of the literate, well-off, cultivated men and women of the Tyndale family's acquaintance were sympathetic to the Lollards. This must have impressed the young Tyndale.

And then there was the troubling state of the opulent, corrupt Roman Church. The great who held the high offices of Catholicism generally came from the same families or family webs which provided the aristocracy. The majority of clergy were poorly prepared. The general state of learning among the clergy was pitiful, but officially tolerated. It gave those in charge no unease.

There is a report from Gloucestershire from about 15 years after Tyndale's martyrdom. Under Bishop Hooper it found 'negligence and ungodly behaviour of the monasteries of Gloucestershire . . . inhospitable, non-resident, inefficient, drunken and evil-living incumbents found in every deanery'.

In Wotton-under-Edge alone, it was recorded that nine clergy did not know how many commandments there were, 33 did not know where they appeared in the Bible, 168 could not repeat them, ten could not remember the Creed, 39 did not know where the Lord's Prayer appeared in the Bible, 34 did not know its author, and ten were unable to recite it.

Such maggots of negligence were fattened on what increasingly appeared to be the rotting corpse of a once vital apostolic mission to England. This was not unnoticed. To the woollen merchants, as to others, the Church was ready for clipping.

In 1506, when he was 12, William Tyndale (or Hychyns as he was sometimes recorded in the general confusion of surname certainties at the time) was sent to Magdalen College School in Oxford. He would have had private tuition up to that age. From his phrases and usages he appears to have developed a lifelong affection for his county as he did for his country.

Magdalen was, alongside Winchester and Eton, one of the three most influential schools in England. The school was distinguished by its adoption of newer methods of teaching. But the common medieval educational structure remained. In the first form, they learned the eight parts of speech and pronunciation of Latin; in the second, to speak

Latin, and on to grammar, then on further to the classical authors, Terence, Virgil, later Cicero, Sallust and Caesar; then on to Ovid and turning verse into prose and back again, and Aesop, whose ease seems to have influenced the boy Tyndale.

School hours were 6 a.m. to 9 a.m., followed by breakfast; 9.45 to 11 a.m., then dinner; and 1 p.m. to 5 p.m. – possibly four or five days a week. He was well grounded in the habit and demands of hard study.

At that time Oxford was thought to have surpassed Paris to become the leading university in Europe. There were 12 colleges, and the architectural masterpiece of the School of Divinity had just been built, as had Magdalen Tower. As he roved around the school and college, the young Tyndale must have felt the excitement of this place: the ruling seat of learning in all England.

And yet. Already Tyndale is critical and, characteristically, it is on one specific point: Scripture. Throughout his life he was to criticize the Oxford curriculum. The insistence on drumming in a knowledge of Latin by way of classical authors at school and at university left what in Tyndale's view was the crux of learning, the Scriptures, far too late. The classical 'pagan' authors received far more attention than the Scriptures.

He never ceased to maintain that the essential study had to be the Scriptures. Only in the Scriptures could the truths of life through God and Christ be discovered and acted on. Oxford, he thought, wasted valuable time on Roman literature which was useful for fluency in Latin but irrelevant to the main purpose.

He received his BA in 1512, his MA in 1515, and by then he was already writing. And defining himself – turning the boyhood intoxication with the Saxon English Christian King Athelstan into a vision which only strengthened year on year. It was a profound and, it was to prove, life-draining, life-threatening, lifelong vision.

He was already working on his translation when he moved to Cambridge some time between 1517 and 1521.

Two mighty forces dominated his intellectual, spiritual and essential landscape at that time. The first was his discovery of the translation of the New Testament into Greek by the celebrated Dutch humanist and scholar Erasmus: a eureka moment for Tyndale. The second was the Ninety-Five Theses of Luther of 1517 condemning the Catholic Church, the eruption of centuries of deeply entrenched and, as Luther saw it, decaying and diseased Roman Catholicism.

Tyndale embraced both men yet steered his own course through the turbulence. It was a vicious period of ideological conflict whose consequences are still with us.

2

A prophet without honour

William Tyndale wrote little about himself in the revealing personal way of a diary or a contemporary memoir. It was rarely done in his day and he was a man of modesty. Foxe (who wrote at enormous length about these times, especially in his contested but invaluable *Book of Martyrs*) describes him as 'a man of most virtuous disposition and of life unspotted'. A young Thomas More wrote of him as 'a man of right good living, studious and well learned in scripture and in divers places in England . . . very well liked and did a great good with preaching'. We are told, again by Foxe, of his ever-increasing 'knowledge of tongues' and of the Scriptures 'whereunto his mind was singularly addicted'.

There are gaps which can be sketched in with sensible speculation, although evidence is scarce. It is likely, for instance, that he stayed on at Oxford after 1515 when he got his MA, teaching as well as continuing his own studies. It is all but certain that in 1512 he read the short and extremely influential book *De Copia* by Erasmus, which outlined the devices of rhetoric, or the art of persuasion. This, taught in schools throughout the century, according to the historian David Daniell, led to the later emergence of the rich fluidity of English prose and poetry for the next one and a half centuries.

De Copia taught variety and encouraged subtlety. One famous practice lesson illustrated 150 different ways of writing 'your letter delighted me very much'. Erasmus's work fed and aided an intensifying excavation of the depths and the potential of an English language which had been for so long degraded and oppressed. Chaucer, Malory, Langland and a few others had come through, and Wycliffe with his banned Bible, but Tyndale seized on the language as capable of expressing all that needed to be said on any subject and went on to prove his conviction. The influence of *De Copia* in the schools of England was such that it was said, 'without Erasmus, no Shakespeare' (equally, 'without Tyndale, no Shakespeare').

The influence of Erasmus, the great humanist scholar from Rotterdam, was vital. First, this widely acclaimed scholar believed that the Bible ought to be available in the words of the people. Second, his own writing, especially his Greek New Testament (1516), directly encouraged Tyndale's own mission. Erasmus believed that to get at the truth you had to cut through the Latin and search out the original Greek in which the New Testament was written. This Tyndale did. He was enraptured by it, translating it himself twice and using it as an example to delve even deeper when later he taught himself Hebrew.

The determination to give English people the Bible in their own tongue was strengthened, I think, by Tyndale's unquestionable patriotism. He was both angry and ashamed that so many of the major languages in 'Europe' had Bibles in their local tongues. England was the exception. The dunce? The sluggard? The fearful one? All and any of these. All added, I am sure, to that fire in Tyndale's mind that burned to make the Scriptures part of his native common tongue.

Erasmus had taught at Cambridge, leaving there in 1512, and although there is no conclusive proof that Tyndale moved across from Oxford to spend time there, it is very likely that he did, and may have met Erasmus there. Certainly many Cambridge scholars had done so, and Tyndale would surely have encountered Cambridge men who were Protestant by 1518.

Above all, it was either here or in Oxford that the name and power of Martin Luther rose up like a mythical god from the deep. He was to challenge all the structures and malpractices of Catholic religion, to sweep corruption aside, drown it in his violent logical outpouring of words, and in a unique storm, try to blow it clean by force of argument.

Fear of Luther at first outstripped support for him. His teachings helped provoke peasants' revolts in which thousands were killed and the established foundations of European rule were rocked. What had this man unleashed? Luther called for an end to the Papacy, to the hierarchy of religious command, and to penitence, pilgrimages and purgatory. It was an apparatus built up over centuries, he wrote, solely to enrich those in command and degrade those in dependence.

It was Luther's attack on the sale of indulgences, by which you bought your way out of purgatory by donating money to the Church – the Papacy's prime money-earner, which made the Papal forces realize that not only their indulgent practices but their livelihoods were at stake. It was war. Tyndale over the next few years was to be sucked into the heart of it.

The opening shots against Lutheranism in England began in May 1521, when Cardinal Wolsey (another brilliant Magdalen College scholar) presided over a burning at St Paul's Cross. He sat under a canopy of gold, deliberately flaunting the privileged riches decried by the monk Martin Luther.

We are told that bishops and ambassadors were present to witness this burning of Luther's books, most of which had been bought especially for the occasion. There must have been enough in the bookshops of London to feed the bonfire (although it was not entirely beyond Wolsey to have shipped in extra stock to keep the flames leaping). But Wolsey wanted to show his Catholic King, Henry VIII, who was to become a passionate Defender of the Faith – he was given that title by the Pope – that the true Church would easily dispose of this rabble-rousing, uncouth German monk. First burn the books and then . . .

From an English Catholic perspective, Luther was the monstrous beast out of its lair, stalking Germany and threatening the rest of 'Europe', leading an army of arguments marching on Rome, destroying the guardians of the Old, proclaiming the virtue and the certain truth of the New. His revolutionary cry was that we can be saved by faith alone.

Uproot all these cheating and footling tricks and bribes of salvation. Your soul is not in the hands of this bejewelled and strangulating infestation of lies at the false heart of Roman politics. It is in the clear simplicity of grace. Through grace, through faith in God, through belief in this, you will be saved at the last. No need any more for all the pomp and circumstance of the Vatican and its multi-channelled control system. No need to cower before rules invented to make money for idle monks, absentee priests, for aural confessors, ignorant churchmen, waddling bishops and all the company of that Roman haven. Be free. Speak directly to your God in faith and he will listen and you will be saved.

What the authorities saw was their own Armageddon. Once people were freed from the grip of the Church, what next? Clearly – the State. And that is what happened. There was a riot of uprisings – often bunched together as peasants' revolts (the usual inaccurate and dismissive phrase when any uprising occurred – implying the revolt of the ignorant, the poor and the worthless). The Church and the Catholic States were in it together from the start. Lutheranism had to be eradicated: the ideology, the man and his followers.

Where was Tyndale in all this? He was now utterly devoted to learning Greek to such a pitch of accomplishment that he could translate the Greek New Testament – the words of Christ and the apostles – into English. This he believed would unlock truth for the English. That resolution hardened. Time had to be found to achieve this at the level he demanded of himself.

Meanwhile, out in the wider world, he was increasingly associated with Protestant sympathizers. He was still, in the 1520s, living in a country obstinately, dutifully, devoted to all that the Roman Catholic Church stood for and praised. The reform movement, despite its long fertilization by the Lollards, was small and without representation in any of the halls of power. It was a pact among equals which became easy to turn into a pack to be hunted down. But Tyndale did not waver in his support.

His next move is well recorded and wholly unexpected.

* * *

He went back to Gloucestershire. At Little Sodbury Manor he became a tutor to the children of Sir John Walsh, a wealthy and important man in the county. The Walsh family were known to the Tyndales. He was among company he liked and in the countryside to which he had returned again and again in the long vacations from Oxford. It is not too much to assume that it was this countryside to which he would return in his imagination in the many fraught foreign years ahead.

Tyndale was, as has been recorded, addicted to his work. He could have earned a living teaching at Oxford or Cambridge. Presumably his family, who were always ready to support him, would have done so in 1521. Instead he had, I think, found the perfect place to devote himself to the study of Greek.

He needed substantial solitude – which he got in his rooms in the roof of the manor house. He seems to have decided that he would be better off at this stage not to be in the midst of feverish debates on Luther, Wolsey, Catholicism . . . A little light tutoring would earn him an honest wage and the hospitality of the house, and his own native habitation, he might have thought, would nourish him in the compelling labour of translation. It suited him down to the ground.

More surprising is the evidence we have that he preached in nearby Bristol on a spot called St Austin's Green, in front of the Augustinian priory. This spot was available to all, and brings out a strand in Tyndale's character which up until now we have not seen. A young Thomas More commented on it. Open-air preaching was traditional especially in areas where a challenging sermon was welcome. You could argue that in doing this Tyndale placed himself in direct descent from John Ball, the hedge priest who with Walter Tyler in 1381 led the biggest popular rebellion (per head of population) that this country has ever seen. John Ball railed against the Pope, the bishops and the wealth and privilege of the Church. For this he was imprisoned three times and excommunicated twice, once by a court whose judges included the King of England and the Archbishop of Canterbury. He was feared to such an extent that in the end he was hung, drawn and quartered.

Speaking at large, in the freedom of the open air, unconfined by buttressed buildings and conforming churches, bolder preachers could get away with far more than the Bible-bound servants of the Church within walls. Tyndale sought out those who wanted to hear sermons that were outside the prescribed order of things. It was not without risk.

His sermons would have been in English. We have no idea of their content. The excitement of taking on all-comers on the Green would surely have encouraged some licence, and that being so there is not much doubt that Tyndale would have taken advantage of it. He could have slipped in English quotations from the Lollards' (Wycliffe's) Bible. He could have taken up other gobbets in English as lessons for the day. He could well have commented on the biggest revelation of all, to which his new Greek took him directly in Paul – justification by faith. Unorthodox, dangerous, even heretical? This was the beginning of his subversive reputation.

For here, at Sodbury, we discover that inside the scholar, who would master eight languages and have knowledge of others, who would later teach himself Hebrew and be reported by his friends as working at his translation for 12 to 15 hours a day, there was audacity, even recklessness.

This is confirmed by an account of one of the finest illuminations of the young Tyndale's character which occurred in the beautiful Cotswold stone manor house in which he lodged. It was an argument at the dinner table.

Sir John Walsh was a generous host. His table was renowned for its food and wines. He was lavish in his entertainment of local divines and he and his wife appear to have enjoyed learned disputation around his table. The story, well sourced and detailed, leads us to the first recorded step which set Tyndale on the way to becoming, in effect, an outlaw.

* * *

There was a great deal of talk in England at that time about Luther and Erasmus of Rotterdam. Tyndale gave no quarter in these discussions; whatever the rank of the speaker he would, if challenged, haul out the Scriptures and prove the person wrong. If what was proposed was not in the Scriptures, it had no value. Add to this his agreement with Luther on the matter of Pope, purgatory and pilgrims, and lively arguments must have disturbed what should have been a gentle subsidence into vinous Gloucestershire complacency.

On this occasion, we are told, these prominent churchmen – including abbots, deans, archdeacons and doctors – 'waxed weary and bore a secret grudge against Master Tyndale'. (This story, told by Richard Webb of Chipping Sodbury, was put down by Foxe.) This too-clever young man disturbed them.

The aggrieved diners subsequently invited Sir John and Lady Walsh to a banquet without Tyndale and laid out their complaints. When the couple came back to the manor house, Tyndale was presented with their grievances and answered them all. Lady Walsh, however, responded with what she considered to be the end to the matter by saying, 'There was one doctor among them who may spend one hundred pounds by the year, another three hundred, and' (to Tyndale) 'what think ye, were it reason that we should believe you before them, so great, learned and beneficed men?'

Tyndale took his time in replying, and translated one of Erasmus's shortest books, *Enchiridion Militis Christiani* (*The Manual of a Christian Soldier*), to justify his views: how to put on the armour of God and avoid the temptation of the flesh; be moderate in all things – eating, drinking – and have great knowledge of the classics and above all Scripture. At that stage Tyndale would have agreed that 'Erasmus laid the egg that Luther hatched'. In this work Erasmus attacks church practices (with his usual fence-sitting tact – no real offence is given to the well bred and well read), like the sale of relics and the worship of saints. But he lays into monks who 'live in idleness' and are 'fed off other men's liberality'.

We are told that Sir John and Lady Walsh were convinced by Erasmus's arguments and Tyndale's high character. The local leaders of the Church were no longer invited to Sodbury Manor. This in several ways – for the luxury of it, for the exclusiveness of it, for the company of other eminents and the friendship of good Sir John – was a deprivation angrily received. They would be revenged.

The crucial importance of all this is that Tyndale was to be fingered by these men as a heretic – the worst crime in the Church and open, if proved, to the ultimate punishment. Tyndale later writes in his prologue to his translation of the Pentateuch, 'I was so turmoiled in the county where I was that I could no longer there dwell . . .'

He was brought to examination in a local bishop's consistory and accused of being 'an heretic in Sophistry, an heretic in Logic, an heretic in Divinity'. Tyndale responded by saying, 'I am content that you bring me where you will into any county within England, giving me ten pounds a year to live with. So you bind me to nothing but to teach children and preach.' And, we can assume, although he did not say it in his defence, continue to study and to write. Tyndale later reported that he was threatened and reviled; the officer, he said, 'rated me as if I had been a dog'.

He was not charged. The assumption must be that they could not find sufficient corroborative damning evidence. He was not found to be a heretic, and Tyndale's conclusion was that the root of the matter was the clergy's ignorance of the New Testament. But this encounter tainted him, and was to be the flame that lit the fire that would send him into exile.

And there was one final incident, again reported by Richard Webb.

Still in Gloucestershire, where his nest had turned out to be full of vipers, he was again in company with some local learned divines, one of whom said, 'We were better without God's Law than the Pope's.'

Tyndale was incensed. 'I defy the Pope,' he said, 'and all his laws and if God spare my life ere many years I will cause a boy that driveth the plough shall know more of the Scripture than thou dost.'

Although it took some months fully to bite, the die was cast. He became an enemy of the established Church and its powerful defenders and dependants.

In those few words we have the essence of Tyndale – wholly unafraid to stick to his views and express them with public force. The choice of the ploughboy is an aspect of his genius. A ploughboy opened up the land to feed the people, a mundane marvel task like those of the apostles, in stories and in myths; he was an innocent. Above all, the ploughboy was illiterate. This was for him a key incentive.

Tyndale would write a Bible to be read aloud so that everyone who had ears to hear would learn at last the messages in the Scriptures. In doing this he would employ a style so brilliantly adapted to his aim that it would be criticized as being artless, too simple, too common. In truth, it was constructed with mastery. He made a lasting new language from and for the common people of England.

* * *

Tyndale's move to London in 1523 appears to have been forced on him. The examination at the bishop's court – more of a trial, and something of a show trial – and the violent words of the bishop's chancellor had an effect. The church establishment in that part of Gloucestershire, scorned and rightly so by Tyndale for its ignorance and unforgivable lack of any real knowledge of the New Testament, had bitten back. They had used the word 'heresy' – a contaminating association. Although he had outwitted them this time in his own quiet, thought-through way, the slur would fester.

Years later, Thomas More would refer to it as part of his demonization of Tyndale. Perhaps Tyndale's employers thought he had become a liability. Or he wanted to relieve them of the responsibility they felt towards him. Perhaps in some way he thought he ought to behave like a Christian knight and put on his own armour. He was always courageous. For whatever reason, he left for London.

We may assume that his study of Greek had made progress and that he was some way towards translating Erasmus's Greek into English. Before he went to London his Greek was good. Tyndale was a man of decisions and Erasmus had convinced him that the path to the truth of the Scriptures was to study Greek. So that is what Tyndale did.

He arrived in London, outstanding scholar as he already was, with the innocence of the traditional country boy seeking his fortune in the big city. His faith was strong and would always stay secure in the purity to which he directed it. He was happy in any company of elite biblical scholars. He had a loyal family and a plan. He was most likely already at work on his own translation of the New Testament.

Erasmus, whose policy towards anyone who gave him board and gainful employment was, as Tyndale wrote, to make 'of little gnats great elephants', had nevertheless convincingly praised the new Bishop of London, Cuthbert Tunstall. He was another Oxford man, studying there with More a decade or so before Tyndale. He too was a Greek scholar. At the time, that connection would have increased Tyndale's hopes that a meeting with Tunstall might be the first rung on one of many ladders in the abundant opportunities provided by the Church. Under Tunstall's reign as Bishop of London no heretic was burned, despite his relentless opposition to Luther and all his works. Only the books were burned. Thomas More, in the days before his fanaticism, refers to Tunstall in his most famous book *Utopia* as 'an excellent person . . . his learning and moral character . . . are too remarkable for me to describe adequately, and too well known to need describing at all'.

Even allowing for the fashion for flattery of the day, there is enough in Tunstall's life and work even before he became Bishop of London to single him out as a man who would listen to and welcome a scholar such as Tyndale. 'Then thought I,' Tyndale wrote, 'if I might come to this man's service, I were happy. And so I gat me to London . . .'

It was a London of hectic commerce, with a court under Henry VIII which was beginning to catch its volatile King's growing anxiety about his lack of an heir; a medieval city in many ways, stinking in its streets, brutal in many of its pastimes, often subject to plagues, but vigorous and self-confident. Yet, when Tyndale arrived in 1523, an Anti-Christ was shadowing London. Luther.

By 1523 Luther was a menace at large and an unmistakable threat to the Church and State throughout 'Europe'. Although England was stoutly Roman Catholic – and, in its majority, was to remain so well after Henry VIII's death – the flame of Luther's arguments had lit a fire. A core of determined and influential men in London and the court fought fire with fire. There was the Wolsey book-burning, already noted; that was just the beginning.

Wolsey was also an Oxford man; he had been at Magdalen College a few years before Tyndale. This son of a butcher had left Oxford in a glory of scholarship to which he soon added political skills which saw him soar to the heights of authority, second only to the King himself. Wolsey wanted to take the next step and become Pope. He knew that to do that he had to serve two courts – that of King Henry VIII and the Vatican.

When Tyndale arrived in London, Wolsey was doing this with dedication and cunning. He had helped steer his King to publish a violent attack on Luther, which had earned Henry the swagger title of 'Defender of the Faith', which he cherished. Now he was on the hunt for heresy. He would winkle out Lutherans however they masked themselves in apparently harmless dissent. He would prove to a panicking Christendom across 'Europe' that he was the man to eradicate this potentially fatal disease, which threatened the authority and wealth of the sacred traditional Church of God and the Pope. In the process, Wolsey became 'the best hated man in England'.

Tyndale's timing for seeking a meeting with Bishop Tunstall may have been unlucky. In April 1523 Wolsey summoned the only Parliament to meet between 1515 and 1529 and Tunstall was called on to address it. This preoccupied him, and his Palace, we are told, was greatly overcrowded. In that context Tyndale's reputation must have been high for him to be so civilly received by Tunstall at all.

Tyndale's report of the encounter has no reproach in it. Tunstall said that 'his house was full, he had more than he could well find, and advised me to seek in London, where he said I could not lack a service'. Tyndale added, seeing through this courtesy, 'I understood at the last that there was no room in my Lord of London's Palace to translate the New Testament.'

Tunstall's political manners were perfect. His religious strategy was clear. The troublemaker, the possible heretic from Gloucestershire, was not to be encouraged. London was now in a war of words and Tyndale's contribution was not welcome. Tyndale was later to call Tunstall 'a ducking hypocrite made to dissemble'.

Tyndale was to stay in London another year. Presumably he continued on his translation of the Greek into English; he preached in churches. He found no other work. Not only was there no room in the Bishop's Palace to translate the New Testament – he concluded that 'there was no place to do it in all England'.

So England alone in 'Europe' would be the only country without a Bible in its vernacular tongue. In Germany alone, by 1522 – the date of Luther's New Testament in

German – there had already been 14 versions, starting in 1466. And France, Italy, Spain . . . the Czechs, the Dutch . . . all had own-language Bibles.

In London Tyndale saw the 'pomp of prelates', the boasting of preachers and other things 'of which I defer to speak', and he made the decision which changed his life. It also changed the English language and influenced the English tongue wherever it went for the next 500 years.

Tyndale had not been persecuted in London – the fury of the anti-Reformation movement was not yet in its full force – but he saw himself ostracized and barred from any office, or any educational or tutoring work which would sustain him. He was approaching 30, and the ambition he had nourished since childhood had never abated. It had matured into a passion for revealing the truth which he would never relinquish, even if it meant embracing self-exile. This is what he did.

As he sailed down the Thames to find the freedom to do his work, he could not know that he would never again see England. His only companion was his 'unconquerable mind'.

3

The New Testament of 1526

He made for Germany. There, although there were dangers, English texts could be printed, distributed, freed at last from the catacombs of lines in Latin, dead to most of the world. In Germany there were numerous printing presses, far more than in laggardly London. And if the German cities failed him, he could always move into the Low Countries, where yet again printing flourished. When Caxton opened his press, the first in London, in 1476, there were already presses in 70 European towns in eight European countries. Tyndale saw a land of Canaan, gathered some funds from friends, packed his library and his freshly written manu-scripts and sailed towards mass publication.

Cologne was his first known destination. He must have known or soon mastered German. It became one of the eight languages in which he was fluent and it is not to be doubted that he was soon at ease in the new country's tongue.

Tyndale worked at the printing house of Peter Quentell. Quentell was a risk-taker. Cologne was strongly Catholic and he knew the odds. Tyndale's assistant was a friar, William Roye, who had been to Wittenberg University and with whom Tyndale was not entirely happy; but the two men got on with it in this efficient, clanking, cold, techno-logically up-to-the-minute printers' shop.

So, unfortunately, did others. John Dobneck, an English-man supervising the printing of his own works, became friendly with his German printers. While drunk, they told Dobneck that England would soon be Lutheran, as two Englishmen were printing off 3,000 copies of the Lutheran New Testament in English. Dobneck went off to a Cologne senator, Herman Rinck, known to be acquainted with Henry VIII, and Rinck got the authority to raid the printing shop, but somehow Tyndale got wind of it. It was the first of several episodes where Tyndale behaved with the speed and daring of a special agent. He found time to secure the pages printed so far (up to Mark's Gospel), and his study books, race to the Rhine and be on a boat headed for the town of Worms before his pursuers reached Peter Quentell's press.

The independence of many of the numerous German city states meant that Tyndale could start again. If he had been unaware up to now of the danger of his enterprise, he was no longer in any doubt. Boundaries would not stop the search and destroy of Henry VIII and Wolsey's ferocity. He found another printer in the city of Worms.

* * *

He is known to have sought help from Luther's German translation. Yet from the beginning, as David Daniell points out in great detail, his own was already an essential distance away from Luther. Here is an example from the Sermon on the Mount. A literal translation of Luther's Matthew reads:

> When he the people saw, ascended he up a mountain and sat himself and his disciples stepped to him and he opened his mouth, taught them, and said 'Blessed are they that spiritually poor are because the heavenly Kingdom is theirs.'

Tyndale's version is:

> Seeing the crowd, he went up into a mountain and when
> he was set, his disciples came unto him and he opened his
> mouth and taught them, saying 'Blessed are the poor in
> spirit, for theirs is the Kingdom of Heaven.'

This is not in any way to disparage the German or to detract from the volcanic influence of Luther. Yet, right away, Tyndale is finding ways with words and rhythms which flow from his many linguistic tributaries and cohere into what were to become (especially in the second edition of 1534) the foundational patterns of what can be called modern written English.

Some language scholars claim that the Sermon on the Mount could be dependent on Tyndale's translation of the Greek alone. Some claim the same prime place for the Latin Vulgate or Luther's German. But what is already happening, I think, is that Tyndale is blending all of them into his own flowing English voice.

This first edition of Tyndale's New Testament is not that with which we are most familiar. That is the 1534 edition, which was much more influenced by the Greek and the Hebrew underlying the Greek. But still this 1526 version is far in advance of Wycliffe's (1380s) valiant effort, and despite its several sources, this translation already shows enough of what will become the basis for the King James Bible.

Take just one paragraph in Matthew in the 1526 edition, from the end of the story about the hiring of labourers for a day's work in the vineyards. Hired at different times through the day, even up to the eleventh hour, each labourer was promised a penny for their work. When the wage was paid out, those hired first supposed they should receive more . . . and they grudged against the good man of the house, saying 'these last have wrought but one hour, and thou has made them equal unto us which have borne the burden and heat of the day.'

He answered to one of them, saying 'friend, I do thee no wrong. Didst thou not agree with me for a penny? Take that which is thy due and go thy way. I will give unto this last, as much as to thee. Is it not lawful for me to do as me listeth with mine own? Is thine eye evil because I am good? So the last shall be first and the first shall be last. For many are called but few are chosen.'

Already we have the new voice of England. In those few lines we see its strengths. It is most memorable in its old English monosyllables: 'so the last shall be first and the first shall be last'; 'take that which is thy due and go thy way'; the 'heat of the day'. And its proverbial mystery, 'For many are called but few are chosen.'

And the democratic morality is resolute: the householder made an equal bond with all the hired men and with all the hired men he kept the equal bond. With just the briefest lapse out of the monosyllabic certainty, he writes: 'Is thine eye evil because I am good?' Here at last was meat for the deepest debates in taverns, in the backs of churches, in any gathering: for those were the words of the Son of God, wholly comprehensible but also open to exploration. Instead of a duty to obey he gave his countrymen and women the freedom to understand. And the 1534 edition will provide more proofs.

His imagination can be radical. For instance, he challenges the notion that Peter has been given the keys to the heavenly kingdom, and that the Pope is the direct heir of Peter; and therefore only through obedience to the Pope can eternal life be unlocked. He points out that the keys go not to the Pope but to each believer who confesses that Jesus is 'the Christ, the Son of the living God'. Another wound in the side of Rome. It is, Tyndale points out (from the Greek of Erasmus), Peter's confession of faith which is 'the rock' on which his Church is built.

His preface, written in 1525, speaks for ordinary people with touching and resolute transparency. To his readers, he suggests,

> if they perceived in any places that I have not obtained the very sense of the tongue, or meaning of the scripture, or have not given the right English word, that they put to their hands to amend it, remembering that so is their duty to do.

It is, in its treatment of sacred literature, unique. They are the words of the Scriptures but they are sacred only in so far as they are seen to carry the truth. That truth is not a monopoly. People are urged to contribute. It is their Bible. Tyndale too would contribute and refine it, as he did over the next eight years.

Boldest of all was his confidence. English had been dismissed as a language unfit for sacred matters. Those in authority damned it as a language of no gravity, no tradition, above all no holiness. God spoke Latin. So did Moses and the apostles. No longer. Not in Tyndale's book.

With this preface, and the New Testament published in 1526, Tyndale's name was entered into the lists as a prime heretic: the English Luther, one who had attacked the roots of Christianity and therefore deserved the heaviest punishment.

A central point being made by Tyndale was that Christians should not be organized into a pyramid of privilege, but should be a 'congregation'. This is how he translated the

Greek word *ekklesia* – hitherto translated as 'Church', with all that implied. For Tyndale there must be no such structural hierarchy. 'Congregation' meant that there was no distinction between worshippers. All the trappings of entitlement were toppled by this insistence on that one word: and that one word inflamed the fears of an ecclesiastical establishment deeply committed in its self-serving, self-enriching, socially advantageous organization. To Tyndale, differences which popes and ecclesiastical commentators over the centuries had staked out on earth did not apply to Christ's true earth or to God's heaven.

In this preface, Tyndale threw down his gauntlet. Christ and his words secure us. 'He that believeth in me, shall never more die.'

Once again, it is essential to emphasize that the fate of the soul was believed to be the work of a life, however foreign or curious that might seem to us today. Tyndale is giving to his countrymen the means to understand that, fully and authoritatively. They were now equal before the Testament, and from this would later grow the ideal of mass democracy. Equal before God. Equal before all men.

At the end of the prologue to the Cologne New Testament, before he escaped to the city of Worms, is a resounding declaration of his own reliance on and utter devotion to the love of God. What shall separate us from it, he asks, and answers (quoting St Paul's Epistle to the Romans, chapter 8):

> I am sure that neither death nor life, neither rule nor power, neither present things, nor things to come, neither high nor low, neither any creature is able to separate us from the love of God which is in the Christ Jesus our Lord.

* * *

So with another brave German printer, Peter Schoeffer, in 1526 Tyndale and his assistant Roye succeeded in producing a complete edition of his New Testament. It did not have anything of the size and pomp of the few pages rescued from Cologne. Those had been copied in style from the monumental translation by Luther. Either Tyndale's funds had been depleted or he made the political decision to go for a version which could and did have practical advantages: easy to carry, easy to conceal.

Thousands of copies were printed. It must have been an exhilarating moment. His reaction reveals his innocence. There was the regular oscillation in his state, between the sharp, unafraid, fast-thinking survivor and the Bible-bound boy whose lifelong ambition was now fulfilled. He genuinely believed that his work was done. Surely no one would be so 'bedlam mad' as to keep the people of England in dark ignorance when they could have access to the true light by listening to or reading the Word of God.

He believed utterly that as soon as this New Testament reached his homeland, all would be revealed and all would be well. How could it not be? It would be staring them in the face. The rumblings, persecution, the increasing violence against English Lutherans cannot have been unknown to him, but he was armed with an innocence, a purity of heart which he never lost.

There is only one complete copy of that 1526 New Testament still in existence. Others have lost a page here, been despoiled there. Out of all the thousands, one. It is in Stuttgart, in an immense library of Bibles – shelves, corridors, paths, highroads of Bibles, all catalogued and cared for in Luther's land.

My initial reaction to Tyndale's Bible was just a tinge of disappointment. So small. It could fit in an inside jacket pocket. And so plain, unprepossessing, it could have been anything at all. Nothing said, 'I am the way, the truth and the light.' Yet as I sat and was allowed to turn the pages, I was moved not only by the struggle that had gone into the production of this wallet-sized volume, but by the course it would take and the majestic way its influence would grow through the next five centuries.

And then its very modesty struck me as so clever. Of course. This was Tyndale. He refused to put his name or even his initials anywhere in the book. He followed the Christian ideal to do 'good deeds secretly and be content with the conscience of well-doing'.

And there was method in it. Such a book could easily be hidden in the flow of clothes; it would never draw attention to itself; it did not demand to be lodged on a lectern. It was portable, always available, free of elaborate designs on your approval. It was perfect for what Tyndale hoped would be a quiet spiritual revolution. Here it was, 27 books – Gospels, the Acts, 21 Epistles and the Book of Revelation.

But it was dynamite. This little book sitting in the Bible stack of Stuttgart would go out into England and then into the world, opening eyes and hearts; it would be essential in the shaping of the future, it would feed belief and liberate imagination. I held it in one hand, as if weighing it for a moment or two. When my time was up I watched with regret as it went back into its box and to its place among books that over centuries so many had lived by, rejoiced in and suffered and died for.

Tyndale destroyed the certainties of hitherto sacred words. *Ekklesia*, the Church, as has already been noted, was no longer, in his view, a place with a specialist corps of Christians, but a congregation, a gathering of the faithful.

The Celtic preachers who had swept south from Iona into Northumbria in the sixth and seventh centuries found their churches in fields; their pulpits, as Christ did, on a mountainside. Again and again over the centuries – with the Methodists particularly in the influential revivalist movements in America – preachers took to the open air, released believers from the rules and constraints of stone walls and spoke their creed directly as they thought, under the eyes of heaven.

Tyndale also clashed with the Church over the Greek word *presbyteros*, which until 1526 was translated as 'priest'. Priests in the Catholic Church have the role of sacred intervention; they mediate between the believer and God. Tyndale, like other Protestants, believed that there was only one priest: Jesus. He is the intermediary. For 'priest' Tyndale substituted the word 'elder'. These would be the wisest people in the congregation and there to advise. By stripping out the priesthood, he was eviscerating the frontline battalions of the Catholic Church. It was a guillotine and a further step in democratization. This proposed turning the entire structure of the Catholic Church inside out.

And the part played by his translation of the Greek gave it an authority (even more marked in the 1534 edition). The plainness of the printing gave a message of accessibility – away with inessential ornamentation and the extravagances of expensive decorations of these holy words. Scriptural words alone were certain good.

And here we see what was even more evident in 1534, this gift, even genius, for the memorable phrase. In 1526, of many hundreds of telling and perfect fit phrases, and from early Matthew alone, we have: 'a city that is set on a hill cannot be hidden'; 'no man can serve two masters'; 'ask and it shall be given you, seek and ye shall find. Knock and it shall be opened unto you'.

Contemporary scholars are not wholly uncritical of Tyndale's Greek at this stage, but are united in admiration for his profound ability to pluck English meaning from those original Greek biblical phrases, time and again. They also point out his gift for storytelling which, it might be suggested, is rooted in Tyndale's affection for the stories of English history and legend. And the ploughboy was never betrayed. In 1868 Bishop Westcott wrote, 'His influence decided that our Bible should be popular and not literary, speaking in simple dialect (which became mother English).'

It always comes back to his English, whatever the minor faults along the way: 'the signs of the times'; 'the spirit is willing'; 'fight the good fight'. That was the next phase in Tyndale's life. It became a fight to the death.

4

Text and terror

It was done. The New Testament translated by William Tyndale was on its way across the North Sea to the home of its language. Tyndale was 32. His boyhood ambition had been achieved: the English would now be able to read, digest and discuss the Scriptures in English. Freely, equally with any other. He must surely have allowed himself some pause of satisfaction. But the few remarks we have from him do not contain self-congratulation. All we know for sure are two things. First, he set to work, on essays, on a closer study of Greek and on teaching himself Hebrew with the aim of reworking the New Testament and taking on the Old. Second, his New Testament, when it bit into the gathering alarm and even hysteria about an English 'Lutheran' version, and was so eagerly bought, intensified a reign of terror which affected him powerfully as it began to scythe down his friends.

Henry VIII would not tolerate dissent from the Church which had made him 'Defender of the Faith'. His chief adviser, Cardinal Wolsey, acted as his King's most conscientious executioner. He instructed the hitherto moderate Tunstall, Bishop of London, to set up a spy system. This would seek out and destroy the printers of the book and hunt for Tyndale in Germany and the Low Countries. He turned the capital of England into a network of informers. London became a city of snoopers, spies, tell-tales, demonizers.

Later, and intensified by Thomas More, London was to become an oppressive cesspit of persecution, torture, show trials and burning. It paralleled any witch hunt. And as word of it spread abroad – it did not happen on the immediate arrival of Tyndale's book – Tyndale stood helpless in disbelief, I assume, and in despair that the words of God and Jesus Christ could cause such vicious reprisals.

It started calmly enough. Hundreds, perhaps about 1,000 or so New Testaments came across from Antwerp early on as part of a regular cargo brought over for London booksellers. It seems that Tyndale had found wealthy enough sympathizers in England – most likely from his family's connections in the West Country and the wool trade – to make this possible. Estimates of the number of books reaching London in the first four years vary between 3,000 and 6,000. In either case it was an outstandingly large number for that time – telling evidence of the appetite for it.

This gentle flow up the Thames lasted only a short time. Wolsey got the willing bishops to agree that it must be burned. He had already, as described earlier, years before bought up and publicly burned Luther's works. What began to dawn on Wolsey and others was that Tyndale was more dangerous than Luther. He was one of their own. Luther had been the volcano, but now it was clear to the English hierarchy that the lava had spread to England and in English. It threatened; it was passionately feared that it would consume and destroy everything in its burning path.

Bishop Tunstall preached a sermon in St Paul's claiming (as it turned out, absurdly) to have discovered 2,000 errors in Tyndale's translation. This line of attack – that Tyndale was not scholar enough to be trusted with such a sacred work – was to persist.

Wolsey's policy was executed. We are told of 'many hundreds' of Tyndale's New Testaments being burned in Antwerp and elsewhere in the Low Countries. In 1527 Bishop Wareham bought up New Testaments (as Wolsey had bought up Luther) for public burnings. Meanwhile, suspected friends and sympathizers of Tyndale were hunted down. Tyndale himself became a prime outlaw, the chief across the water, while his followers were hounded – mown down in the courts and torture chambers of the capital.

But still the Bibles came in. Loose pages, wrapped in bales of cloth or skins or hides or in sealed barrels of wine or flour bags or inserted inside other books. Smuggling through the words of God and his Son was an ingenious and lucrative trade. And a dangerous one. Tyndale's reputation as a threat to the English State grew.

It was when the burning of books was succeeded by the burning of people, mostly men, that the opposition to Tyndale accelerated from anger to panic, to hysteria, to a sort of madness.

In 1526 and 1527 and for some time afterwards the New Testaments were principally bought and read in London, Oxford and Cambridge, and it is in these three citadels that Wolsey and his successors sought and found their prey. Evidence of any substance soon ceased to matter.

Tyndale's adoption of Luther's justification by faith, of inward purity and not outward show, appealed to many Catholics who were weary of the corruption and, as they saw it, falsities in their religion.

The persecutors began by picking on the weak. Foxe, who is counted reliable here, describes at length the Cambridge bachelor of law, Thomas Bilney. Because of his stature and his insignificance in the greater scheme of things (except as a victim), he was commonly known as 'Little Bilney'. He is described as 'meek and charitable, a simple good soul not fit for this world'. He had discovered St Paul's doctrine of justification by faith and records that he 'leapt for joy' at this 'marvellous comfort'. It was the cornerstone of Lutheranism and Tyndale's Protestantism. He was accused of heresy. This bewildered him and never ceased to bewilder him throughout the succession of bullying trials (he was allowed no witnesses in his defence). His declaration – that Luther was 'wicked and detestable' – was ignored.

He was put in the Tower for a year; when he came out he was seriously distressed, and the harassment did not cease. Eventually, in 1531, wholly innocent, he was burned alive.

By that time, the smell of burning Protestant flesh was not uncommon in this redoubt of Catholicism. The earliest martyr was Thomas Hittin. He was accused of smuggling a copy of Tyndale's New Testament into England, condemned by Archbishop Wareham and Bishop Fisher of Rochester and burned at Maidstone in 1529.

Lists of suspects were drawn up; several dozens were interrogated. Some 'abjured' – swore against what they were alleged to believe in (that is, Protestantism – justification by faith). Often they recanted and later went back to the heresy that condemned them to torture and martyrdom.

John Stokesley (another Oxford alumnus) took over from Tunstall as Bishop of London in 1530. He was an enthusiast for tying people to the stake and burning them alive in public places – both men and women.

If you possessed a copy of Tyndale's work you were likely to be tortured and, depending on the whim of the court, it seemed, burned at the stake. Thomas Durgate, James Bainham, John Bent, Thomas Harding, Elizabeth Barton . . .

A considerable number of those arrested were artisans – listed by Foxe – glaziers, tailors, bookbinders, weavers, tillers, often put in prison and left to languish there for months, or die there. There is a strain of the independent skilled working men here which reaches from the fourteenth-century peasants' revolt to the Dissenters of the eighteenth and nineteenth centuries and on to the trades unionists. Innocent men, women and children were arbitrarily accused and often condemned.

It is at this time that Thomas More – whose duel with Tyndale will be returned to – makes his first appearance. He was a man of European reputation as a humanist, famous for his book *Utopia*, published in 1516, and a close friend of Erasmus. Like Erasmus, in his early adult years he was himself content with, if not zealous about, the aim of translating the Bible into English. He was distinguished as a successful, wealthy lawyer and on his way to the highest office in the land. But early in his anti-Protestantism he showed himself to be vicious, cruel and, as the gentle Charles Lamb later wrote, 'with a malice hyper satanic'.

James Bainham of the Inns of Court was found to be in possession of books by Tyndale. He first abjured and then, in public in St Austin's, carrying Tyndale's Bible, recanted and declared his allegiance to Tyndale, saying that in his previous act of denying Tyndale he had 'denied God'.

Thomas More took him to the prison and torture chamber he had established in the gardens of his house in Chelsea on the embankment of the Thames. According to the contested Foxe, More personally 'whipped him at a tree in his garden, called the Tree of Truth, after sent him to the Tower to be racked ... Sir Thomas More being present himself until in a manner he had lamed him'. For two weeks before his death he was 'scourged with whips to make him revoke his opinion'. This has been doubted by some More-ites along the centuries, but never disproved and there was worse to follow.

But still the Bibles came in. More organized raids on the Steelyard, close along the Thames, a docking station for German goods in particular and suspected of being a hub of smuggling. Arrests, threats, terror . . . Yet still the Bibles came in.

Tyndale's revised 1534 edition was to sell out even faster than the New Testament of 1526. It is safe to assume that each copy was read and listened to by several, sometimes scores of people as the Word took the tide of the time and swept across the land. Tyndale lost friends, he lost people known to him by name and reputation in terms of loyalty and their love of God. That must have made him extremely distressed. As did the public burning of hundreds of copies of the New Testament on the steps of St Paul's. We are told that this burning of the Scriptures shocked him severely. When he heard about the burning of the Bibles, bought in bulk for the occasion by the Bishop of London, Tyndale is reported to have said in defiant response, 'Two benefits shall come thereto. I shall get money of his for these books, to bring myself out of debt and the whole world shall cry out upon the burning of God's word.'

He could have blamed himself; he could have found a way to deny what he was doing and surrender, but there is no evidence that it occurred to him. And why should it? The gesture would have been useless, the 'victory' a mere slip in the march of the words of the Lord. He was called on to do God's work: he had no doubt at all about the supreme value of that. He poured oil on troubled flames.

By now in London he had replaced Luther as the chief and worst enemy of the Pope, the Church and the Crown. Despite being across the water, he now seemed the most dangerous man, a threat to the stability and status quo of his homeland. His absence manufactured rumour, and to the authorities he soon became a satanic ogre.

The fact that he was so elusive, despite the increasing efforts of the spy system, gave him an air of glamorous fearlessness. To slay this one dragon would be to rid the realm of all evil. And his writing in such lucid common-tongued prose gave him a following ever increasing. Although initially few in number, they were strong in conviction and tenacity. He had to be stopped. Burning his books was no permanent solution. Burning his friends and converts was a frenzy that darkened the politics and the State of England, but it was providing new converts as fast as it was murdering the old.

He had to be arrested and destroyed.

This task became a preoccupation of three intelligence agencies: that of the Holy Roman Emperor, that of the Vatican, that of Henry VIII's ministers. Yet such was Tyndale's own intelligence that, with the help of a small web of sympathizers, he was to keep them at bay for over a decade. Only a betrayal led to his capture.

He had help with his work during this period – from George Joye, for instance, and Miles Coverdale. It is doubtful whether their assistance was an addition to his work of translation; more a second head for research, perhaps, a useful, maybe even at times a necessary conversational colleague. Some of these assistants were to rush into print with Tyndale's work after his death, claiming it as their own – claims later routed by close examination of the text.

He began to spend more and more time in Antwerp, where the English House had a powerful presence thanks to the active and important trade in the much-valued English wool. This was to provide protection and some cover over the years. And who but a few knew what Tyndale looked like? We have no clear idea. Holbein did not capture him. There is no evidence that he tried to – Tyndale was well outside that famed circle. Anonymity was a blessing, and being no more than yet another scholar/ priest in a black gown moving unobtrusively through the crowded streets of an Antwerp full of such figures was a perfect public camouflage. And his friendships were few and discreet.

The 1526 publication was his first big statement. He would go on both to revise that New Testament for the defining edition of 1534, and to embark on the Old Testament. Meanwhile, Tyndale the preacher returned to the battle. We have no record of any open-air preaching while he was being hunted down in Germany and the Low Countries. But the preacher would not be denied.

He wrote preaching essays, which added to the turmoil in London. Soon after issuing the New Testament and while still ducking and retaliating to the volleys of disapproval and the threats of extinction from England, he published *The Parable of the Wicked Mammon*. He must have known it would further inflame the already inflamed. It is written in a beautifully learned style but was guaranteed to madden his frustrated tormentors.

The theme of the book is, unsurprisingly, that faith is more important than works. He found all the proofs he needed for this in the Scriptures. But this was the defining English rendition of the war cry of Luther.

The Parable of the Wicked Mammon was a disruptive taunt: Tyndale in the pulpit of his pages goading the gentlemen ecclesiastics of England to a fury. It was the first book of which he claimed authorship. The sermon, after all, was not God's words but his.

He took as his text the parable in Luke in which in effect a wicked steward extricated himself from accusations of inefficiency by smart dealing and was commended. Faith, he then argues, with pile-driving quotations from Scriptures, alone 'brings life, the law and death'. He leans on Luther at the beginning, and then – gathering strength as his own man in this Protestant debate – he develops it in his own fashion.

There are sentences here which could be Tyndale's own Testament. 'Deeds are the fruits of love,' he writes, 'and love is the fruit of Faith.' But the New Testament itself shines through this long essay and is a deliberate part of Tyndale's lifelong plan to bring the Scriptures to the people. Very early on, in the West Country, he had blamed the intransigence of the prelates who were to persecute him on their 'ignorance of the Scriptures'. Going back to the springs and origins of the faith was what he always did, for there was the meaning and purpose of life.

The Parable of the Wicked Mammon was published in Antwerp in May 1528. The reaction in England was extreme. It was claimed to contain dozens of heresies. Sir Thomas More called it 'the wicked book of Mammon'. Wolsey demanded of the Low Countries that they hand over Tyndale. Alongside the New Testament of 1526, *Wicked Mammon* became a book you could be condemned merely for possessing. It became a favourite of enthusiasts for reform and they often suffered for it. John Tewkesbury, a leather-seller of London discovered to have read Tyndale's New Testament and *Wicked Mammon*, was another who was tortured in Sir Thomas More's Chelsea gardens, then put to the rack in the Tower 'until he was almost lame'. He abjured, and turned against Tyndale. Later, when feeling less distraught and recovering from the torture, he turned back to his original views and he was burned alive. His arguments in his defence were said to have been better than those of the bishops.

In London, Bishop Stokesley became a compulsive executioner. Evidence was twisted, answers invented. Tyndale's words were misquoted to serve against him. Under that jolly-looking Tudor, Henry VIII, there was an authoritarian regime with eyes and ears in every tavern, street and congregation. Young men were thrown into deep, stinking, infected dungeons. Tyndale's brother was pursued. Who could be safe was as vital as who could be saved. The capital lived under a canopy of dread.

But for Tyndale and his fellows, this was just the beginning of the struggle to bring truth to England through English.

5

Enemy of the State

At the end of the 1520s there's another story of high adventure in the unquiet life of William Tyndale.

By this time we have him more clearly in our sights. He lived a very frugal life – he ate 'sodden meat' (cheap) and drank simple small beer (cheap again, and purer than water). He received some money from the sale of his books but this would just about cover the printing expenses; otherwise he was reliant on the generosity of acquaintances. From a later letter we learn that his material possessions, including his clothes, were few, well worn and barely adequate for the cold of Antwerp winters. His mission consumed his mind, threatened his health and dominated every hour of his life.

Foxe reports that as he moved printers yet again 'on his way . . . he suffered shipwreck by the which he lost all his books, writings and copies, and so was compelled to begin all again anew, to his hindrance and doubling of his labours'. The effect of this must have been severe. It was the loss of everything that enabled his work, as well as that most recent and hard-crafted work itself.

But he found another ship which took him to Hamburg and with the help of his assistant, Coverdale, he translated 'the whole five books of Moses, from Easter (1529) to December' in the house of a sympathizer – 'a worshipful widow, Mistress Margaret van Emmerson'. We are also told that during these months there was 'a great sweating sickness in the town'. What for many would have been utterly disheartening seems to have been a spur to Tyndale. After this he returned to Antwerp.

Meantime, back in London, while Tyndale was moving on to the Old Testament and ploughing through the works then thought to have been written by Moses, the anti-Tyndale faction was festering and growing into an opposition wider than just that of the Church. It became a matter for the State, and one of the most pressing urgency. In 1529, Henry VIII's desperation for a divorce from Queen Katherine was growing.

He called on Sir Thomas More to lead the attack on Tyndale's Protestant 'heresy', which he saw as a barrier in his negotiations with the Papacy. Wolsey had failed to secure what Henry wanted. He was discarded, and soon after that shame, in 1530, he died. More, who would rise to become the Lord Chancellor, was tasked with demolishing the works of this troublesome priest.

More needed no encouragement. His attacks on Tyndale, together with Tyndale's robust and often withering replies, run to over 750,000 words. We see the malicious, all but insane aspect of the man who was to be made a saint.

More's publication *The Dialogue Concerning Heresies* reveals why he considers Tyndale to be the most dangerous man in Tudor England. I spoke to the Tudor historian John Guy about More in the very chapel, by the Thames, in which More once worshipped. I asked him first what *The Dialogue Concerning Heresies* consisted of.

John Guy explained that More employed one of his usual complicated narrative methods. It purports to be a conversation with someone More calls 'the messenger', with More's usual curlicues, but the blunt theme soon emerges.

This man sympathizes with Tyndale, and More sets out to slaughter his arguments. 'More saw Tyndale,' John Guy said,

> almost in the same way that during the Cold War the Soviet Union and America stared at each other . . . because More argued that if Tyndale was right about authority then half of the institutions of the Catholic Church collapsed . . . authority will be dictated by Scripture but the problem that More saw was – whose interpretation of Scripture would hold sway? You will have chaos.

John Guy then pointed out a passage from More in which this author of *Utopia* predicted what would happen if Tyndale got his way:

> If Tyndale's Testament be taken up then shall false heresies be preached, then shall the sacrament be set at naught . . . then shall Almighty God be displeased, then shall He withdraw His grace and let all run to ruin . . . then will rise up rifling and robbery, murder and mischief, and plain insurrection . . . then shall all laws be laughed to scorn . . .

More was conscious that with Tyndale he was not only fighting the enemy of the Church, he was fighting the prime enemy of the State as well. 'In More's Catholic State,' Guy said, 'the Church and State have to work together. Tyndale was threatening the Church and the peace of the realm.' 'I will follow him,' More said, 'to the World's End.'

The language of engagement between these two could by our standards be viewed as rough. Here is a small sample. More maintained that the only way the Scriptures could be understood was through the teaching of the Fathers of the Church and the priests presiding over the sacraments. And all ordered under Rome. Tyndale thought that even unedu-cated men and women could arrive at their faith without

Little Sodbury Manor, home to the Welch family whose children Tyndale
tutored

Illustration from the beginning of Tyndale's first English translation of the New Testament, 1526

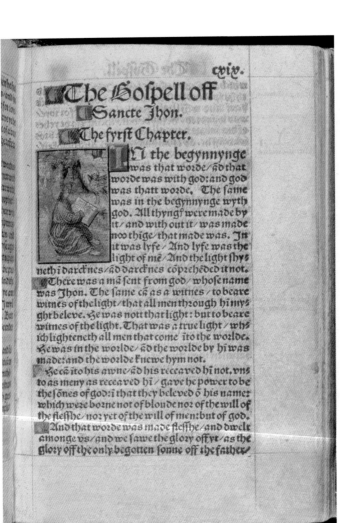

The Gospell off Sancte Jhon.

The fyrst Chapter.

IN the begynnynge was that worde/ãd that worde was with god: and god was thatt worde, The same was in the begynnynge wyth god. All thyngſ were made by it/ and with out it/ was made noo thige/ that made was. In it was lyfe/ And lyfe was the light of me/ And the light shyneth i darcknes/ ãd darcknes coprehended it not.

There was a mã sent from god/ whose name was Jhon. The same cã as a witnes/ to beare witnes of the light/ that all men through hi myght beleve. He was nott that light: but to beare witnes of the light. That was a true light/ which lighteneth all men that come ito the worlde. He was in the worlde/ ãd the worlde by hi was made: and the worlde knewe hym not.

He cã ito his awne/ ãd his receaved hi not, vn to as meny as receaved hi/ gave he power to be the sones of god: i that they beleved õ his name: which were borne not of bloude nor of the will of the flesshe/ nor yet of the will of men: but of god. And that worde was made flesshe/ and dwelt amonge vs/ and we sawe the glory off yt/ as the glory off the only begotten sonne off the father/

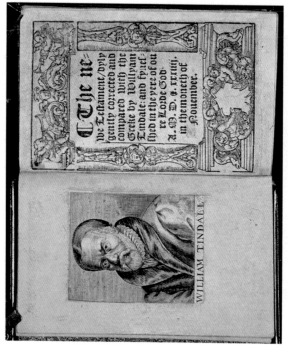

The ne=
we Testament/dyly
gently corrected and
compared with the
Greke by Wyllyam
Tindale: and fyneſ
ſhed in the yere of ou
re Lorde God
A.M.D. & xxxiiij.
in the moneth of
November.

WILLIAM TINDALE

William Tyndale's New Testament, published November 1534, Antwerp

Woodcut depicting the martyrdom and burning of William Tyndale, from Foxe's *Book of Martyrs* (1563)

Portrait of William Tyndale, although there is thought to be
no authentic image of him. By the early seventeenth century,
a false one was in wide circulation, deriving from a portrait
of John Knox from a shop in Fleet Street

Statue of William Tyndale, Victoria Embankment Gardens, London

Melvyn Bragg on the site of the place Tyndale was held before he was put to death in Vilvoorde

the intervention of the Church. Humankind, he thought, was born with a spiritual sense.

More wrote, 'you kissed the arse of Luther . . . the shit devil . . . look, my fingers are smeared with shit when I try to clear your filthy mouth'. There is much, much more of this. Tyndale called More 'a lying Papist' and the Catholic Church, he said, was 'the devil of Satan'.

But then the world turned upside down yet again because Henry VIII, shackled to a wife, Katherine of Aragon, who could not produce a son, in search of an heir and unsatisfied in his lust, had met Anne Boleyn in Hever Castle in Kent and fallen, he asserted, in love. Anne was a Protestant.

* * *

In 1528, Henry VIII appealed to the Pope for an annulment of his marriage to Katherine. He based his claim on a verse in the Book of Leviticus (20.21). He claimed that as Katherine had been married to his late brother and as the Bible did not permit a man to marry his brother's widow . . . The Pope refused him.

In the same year Tyndale published another of his 'sermons' – *The Obedience of a Christian Man*. Anne Boleyn is said to have made sure that a copy found its way into Henry's hands. Suddenly, this Tyndale, this Lutheran dog, seemed to deliver to the Catholic King the political salvation he needed.

In his book Tyndale wanted to enforce the notion of the supremacy of Scripture and defend the supremacy of kings. God, he writes, is the highest authority in the land, but God has made the King in every realm judge over all. And over him there was no judge. Therefore the supremacy is of the King, and not of the Pope. When Henry read this he is reported to have said that this was a book for him and all kings to read. It was the King who wielded the spiritual sword, not the Pope and the bishops, who merely held the temporal sword.

Tyndale's support was a wonderful gift to Henry. And Tyndale declared his personal loyalty to the King. The King's duty, Tyndale writes, is to oversee the Church and reject Papal authority.

But Tyndale was a probing scholar to his nerve ends. Instead of resting on this unexpected but potentially liberating alliance, he pressed on with the arguments about this major controversy, this divorce which rifted through 'Europe'. Two years later he wrote his essay/sermon *The Practice of Prelates*, in which he prods away, further testing the scriptural evidence and, unfortunately for Henry, finding against him.

Henry was basing his annulment campaign on the Leviticus passage which says a man may not take his brother's wife – 'it is an unclean thing'. In *The Practice of Prelates* Tyndale concedes the truth of this but finds other evidence in the Bible saying that a man *should* marry his brother's widow. Tyndale concludes that this is a commandment. Henry is so incensed by this that he has these comments about marriage excised from later texts. Tyndale's name is banned.

Tyndale now concludes that the annulment would lead to anarchy in the kingdom, from which the corrupt clergy would profit.

It seemed that Tyndale's first positive connection with the court would also be his last. His intense research and his unbending search for the truth was simply more important than placating Henry.

And yet . . . there was one more chance. Thomas Cromwell entered the battle.

6

The agony of exile

After the death of Cardinal Wolsey, Thomas Cromwell, who had been Wolsey's right-hand man, stepped into his post and systematically set about erasing much of what Wolsey had done. Cromwell, among so much else that he did, saw that the future was Protestant and carefully steered his volatile King away from Rome.

He faced a tough task. *The Practice of Prelates* had been burned in its hundreds. Tyndale's brother had been arrested and led through the streets to be mocked before being forced to throw his brother's book on the fire outside St Paul's. The King was in desperate haste to marry Anne Boleyn and produce a legitimate heir.

Cromwell decided to try to get Tyndale back to England. It seemed an impossible request – he had to get the King's permission – but we read in the correspondence of the Imperial Ambassador, Chapuys, that he had heard on the

> most trustworthy authority that the King, afraid lest the priest Tyndale still write more boldly against him, and hoping to persuade him to retract what he had already written, has invited him back to England and offered him several good appointments and a seat on the Council.

Tyndale – on the Council! This was an astounding turn-around. One good explanation for this is that the King preferred to have Tyndale in London, in reach and under

51

control rather than abroad unfettered, unleashing scholarly missiles on his native country. Another is that he or Cromwell saw it as a chance to tease him into a trap, seize him for heresy and silence him on the pyres of Smithfield.

Yet there lurks a suspicion that Cromwell might have been up to good. The man he hoped would contact Tyndale was Stephen Vaughan, the King's factor in the Netherlands. Vaughan sought him in Frankfurt, Hamburg and Marberg with no luck.

Vaughan was fully aware of the difficulty. He wrote to Cromwell:

> It is unlikely to get Tyndale into England when he daily heareth so many things from thence that feareth him ... the man is of greater knowledge than the King's highness doth take him for which well appeareth in his works. Would God he were in England.

Vaughan's admiration seems unfeigned. Significantly, he felt that he could relay that to Cromwell without being accused of disloyalty. Tyndale was important. Even more important than Cromwell realized. And wherever he was, his own contacts were keeping him informed of the English martyrs and other suspects.

Yet Vaughan found his man. He reported this in a letter to the King (which would first be read by Cromwell), which also included a transcription he had made of some of Tyndale's *Answer to Thomas More*, 'written in so gentle a style', he said. But the bulk of this letter gives us the most vivid and moving portrait of Tyndale that we have.

On the evening of 18 April 1531, after several intricacies of arrangement, Vaughan was led out of the gates of Antwerp into a field. When we made the film about Tyndale for the BBC, we had a shot at finding the field. Technical problems dictated against evening filming, but we thought we got near it, early on a winter morning, freezing, frost on the trees and on the ground, dawn most cold – the right 'nowhere' place, the crew thought, perfectly chosen by Tyndale for such a perilous assignation.

Vaughan was taken to the spot by an unnamed messenger – and there was this man, alone. 'My name,' he said, 'is Tyndale.' 'Tyndale!' said Vaughan. 'Fortunate be our meeting.' Now, to revert to Vaughan's detailed and convincing account, Tyndale said, 'Sir, I have been desirous to speak to you.' Vaughan replied, 'And I with you, what is on your mind?' 'Sir,' said he,

> I am informed that the King's grace takes great displeasure with me for putting out certain books, which I lately made in these parts, but especially for the book *The Practice of Prelates* whereof I have no little marvel, wherein it I did but warn his Grace of the subtle demeanour of the clergy of his realm towards his person and of the shameful abusions by them practiced, not a little threatening the displeasure of his Grace and in which I showed and declared the heart of a true subject, which sought the safeguard of his royal person and weal of his commons . . .

Two observations. First, how could Vaughan recall in this detail such well-worked sentences – and more to come? The answer has to be that the schooling of the time with its strict reliance on memory and the daily youthful building up of the muscles of recall would have made a skilled diplomat quite capable of this type of feat. Perhaps he made mental notes along the way and had a system of parking them in his brain for later use. Perhaps he kept brief notes undeclared in this exchange. 'I have written to your Grace word for word,' Vaughan wrote to Cromwell, 'as near as I could by any possible means bring to remembrance.'

Second, Tyndale's priority seems to be to stress his loyalty to the King. This is not done cravenly but, characteristically, argued through. Why did the King not recognize a true subject such as Tyndale?

Then Tyndale gives us a picture of his life and of what he has suffered in order to serve his King truly. It is a sad list and one that takes us into the reality of a scholar enduring much deprivation for his mission. He speaks of 'my poverty', of 'exile out of my natural country and bitter absence from my friends', of 'my hunger and thirst, my cold, the great danger wherewith I am everywhere encompassed'; finally, all this he would accept, because he hoped 'with my labour to do honour to God, true service to my Prince and pleasure to his command'.

Therefore, Tyndale asks him, in doing this does he 'not show a pure mind, a true and incorrupt zeal and affection to his Grace to beware of the Cardinal [Wolsey, whose iniquity he shortly after proved]? Does this deserve hatred?' And why (to come to the heart of the matter), 'being a Christian Prince' is he

'so unkind to God which hath commanded His word to be spread throughout the world . . . and say that it is not lawful for the people to have the same in a tongue that they understand because the purity thereof shall open men's eyes to see their wickedness?'

This is Tyndale in full and plain voice. He cannot comprehend what is not the truth. He believes, totally, that the messages in the Scriptures are self-evident and only need to be expressed in incontrovertible arguments to be accepted.

There is no reason to doubt his descriptions of poverty, hunger and fear and again it is typical of the innocence of Tyndale to point it out plainly. It is not that he wants to wring the heart of his interviewer. It is the case as it is.

His last sentence in the previously quoted paragraph is, 'As I now am, very death were more pleasant to me than this life, considering man's nature to be such as can bear no truth.' That is what must have tormented him every day of his life. Why, when the truth was there, when it could be discovered in the very words of God and Christ – why was it not listened to? What sort of world was this? It is the voice of a man in despair.

I have written of the bold, courageous, dedicated man immersed in the scholarship which he loved, and perhaps set out an impression of someone invulnerable. This confession in a field outside the gates of Antwerp, to an emissary of the King, gives us another view. This was a chance, he must have thought, to speak as directly to the King as he would ever be able. Therefore all that would serve would be the truth, about himself, about the King, about human nature.

Vaughan then tried to persuade him to return to England but Tyndale put aside all assurances: promises he was certain would be broken by clergy who would see him as a heretic and act accordingly.

Then, as night crept on, Tyndale left abruptly, and Vaughan made no attempt to follow him, assuming that Tyndale would be returning to Antwerp where his anonymity had protected him for so long. Just as abruptly, Vaughan's letter breaks off – yet he has given us a vivid portrait of an exhausted, dedicated, inspired man.

Vaughan must have expected his letter to be received with some warmth. Instead, Cromwell replied with uncharacteristic confusion of argument which suggests that someone else had had a say in response to the letter.

It was the King. He had found the book *The Practice of Prelates* an abomination. His anger spills all over Cromwell's text. Full of slanders and lies . . . So the King's Highness, Cromwell wrote to Vaughan, 'to advertise you that his pleasure is that you should desist and leave any further to persuade or attempt the said Tyndale to come into this realm'. Whether this extreme language came from Henry himself or from some of his More-following court officials cannot be confirmed.

But what is most strange is the postscript – 125 words by Cromwell himself, going flat against the King's wishes and telling Vaughan to persist, because 'the King's Royal Majesty is so inclined to mercy, pity and compassion'. Was Cromwell making the bait tastier in order to catch his man? Or was he genuinely of the opinion that the King would show mercy were Tyndale to be restored to England? His tenacity at this stage speaks well for his loyal support of Tyndale – and/or of his unremitting determination to get his man.

Vaughan set up another meeting and this, I think, is the most crucial and the most moving. Vaughan read Cromwell's postscript to Tyndale, who was

> moved to take the same very near to his heart, in such wise that water stood in his eyes, and answered 'What gracious words are these! I assure you if it would stand with the King's most gracious pleasure to grant only a bare text of the Scripture to be out and forth among his people, like as is put forward by the Emperor of these parts of other Christian princes, be it of the translation of what person so ever shall please His Majesty, I shall immediately make

faithful promise never to write more, not abide two days in these parts after the same, but immediately to repair into his realm, and there most humbly submit myself at the feet of his Royal Majesty, offering my body to suffer what pain or torture, yea, what death his Grace will, so this be obtained. And till that time, I will abide the asperity of all chances, whatever shall come, and endure my life in as many pains as it is able to bear and suffer.'

There had to be a Bible in English or Tyndale, despite all, would not yield.

This is such a noble speech. From boyhood Tyndale had aimed to help make a Bible in his native tongue for all who would listen or read. From his youth he had bent himself to the task. He had mastered many languages. He had been driven out of his country. He had worked, sometimes for 18 hours a day. He had been harassed and threatened and, as he said in the meeting with Stephen Vaughan, been subject to many privations and hardships.

But he had never given in. Even now, he was working to further polish his Greek and fully learn Hebrew in order to continue his work on the Old Testament and his revising of the New. His work had been acclaimed by those who mattered to him. Almost as a by-product, even an unintended consequence, of his drive to put the Word of God into English, he had created an English not only for his generation, but for all time.

Yet, because he believed the words about the King of England, because he believed in the divine power of the King of England and because he saw himself as a mere labourer, one of many in the field of translation, he would surrender all of it for the plainest version available. His words about torture show how clearly aware he was of the fate back in England of friends, followers and family, and he would also take that on himself.

By this time he would have trusted Vaughan. He would have trusted that the words of the King's mercy were true. He would give all he had – the work he had completed, his future endeavour and his life – for the assurance that God's Word would be made available in English.

That was his final message sent with Stephen Vaughan back to England, while Tyndale returned to Antwerp and waited for an answer.

None came.

7

The New Testament of 1534

Tyndale returned to his work, in daylight and candle-
light, setting himself ever higher goals. The Defender of
the Faith, meanwhile, having spurned the defender of the
Scriptures, lost patience with the Pope over his annulment.
He addressed Parliament in 1531.

Tyrant in constitutional clothing that he was, he told them
what he would do with his future and the future of England,
the Church and the people. He would become 'sole protect-
or and supreme head of the English Church and clergy'. In
effect he became Pope of the Catholic Church in England.
Even though Henry was to remain Catholic in his own devo-
tions, nevertheless he had made the break. He exited.

In the hearts and minds of Protestants there should have
been a sense of victory even though it had been won not by
doctrinal argument but by the monarch's determination to
jettison Katherine and his itch to marry Anne and get an heir.

But he would not budge on the Bible – it must still be in
Latin. Nor would he give up the sacraments, the penance, the
Mass, the confession. Tyndale, through his heroic innocence
and dedication to English Scriptures, had taken the wise
course in staying away. He would have returned to a false
dawn, a show trial, torture – most likely at the hands of Sir
Thomas More in that Chelsea garden – and the funeral pyre.

More would not let up. Tyndale, he wrote, was 'a hell-
hound in the kennel of the devil', 'a drowsy drudge drinking

deep in the devil's dregs', 'a new Judas', 'worse than Sodom and Gomorrah', 'an idler and devil worshipper, worse than a Mahomet', 'discharging a filthy foam of blasphemies out of his brutal beastly mouth'. Tyndale steadily argued that More's Church was not the true Church because it had abandoned the gospel. This intractability seems to have driven More mad.

Yet More's reputation – after his execution – floated far above that of Tyndale's. For the Roman Catholics he was not just a genius (*Utopia*), a gentleman (a Knight and Chancellor of the Duchy of Lancaster); he was sanctified. I am convinced that More's saintly reputation helped cast that of Tyndale into obscurity for centuries. Tyndale's modesty, the King's refusal to hear, say or see his name (after Cromwell's last failed bid to get him back) and the claims by so many others to be the authors of what he, Tyndale, had written, meant he was never truly recognized until the nineteenth century. Even since then it has been a struggle to see him recognized for his greatness. It was More who was widely celebrated as 'the man for all seasons'. Perhaps now that the dark and vicious side of his character has been revealed, that might change. And from the late nineteenth century, scholarship has at last been generous to Tyndale in a fitting return for the fruits of his own scholarship.

But in 1530 he was moving on to the Old Testament and he would translate the first five books – the books of Moses, the core of Judaism, the underpinning of Christianity.

Now his countrymen need not listen to '*in principe creavit Deus caelium et terram*', but

> In the beginning God created heaven and earth, the earth
> was void and empty, and darkness was upon the deep, and

the spirit of God moved upon the water. Then God said, let
there be light and there was light . . .

At last English was in at the creation. He had routed the
idea that English was too rude for Scripture. It could hold
its own with any language.

And, most importantly for Tyndale, at this stage he had
learned Hebrew. Hebrew, he argued, went better into English
than did Latin, and Hebrew had an almost uncanny affinity
with Old English. That way lay the truest possible translation. The Scriptures, the words and the commentaries of
Christ were to be followed at whatever cost: but Genesis and
the other books in the Pentateuch revealed the voice of God.

It was not only new minted words in English he took
from the Hebrew but old proverbs which he conjured up
to make alliance with the Hebrew. And beyond that there
is the strength of Hebrew grammar: 'the beast of the field',
scholars tell us, is an adoption of a Hebrew grammatical
form. Tyndale found a fraternal resource in the Hebrew
which might have reminded him of the country-rustic Old
English of his childhood and long vacations in the Cotswold
farmlands. The small percentage of later embellishments
by the King James scholars often smoothed away Tyndale's
local and Hebrew-sprung prose. When it goes, we miss it. In
Genesis (3.4), 'then said the serpent unto the woman, tush,
you shall not die,' how wicked, how lovely, how remarkable
is that 'tush'. Instead, the Authorized committee put in, 'And
the serpent said unto the woman, Ye shall not surely die.'
Nothing like as vivid or subtly complex in its mix of snake-
charm flattery and a lie. 'Tush' is a sad loss.

These books of the Old Testament are the first translations of Hebrew into English and add yet another layer to

the Latin and Greek – almost in ascending importance of enrichment.

Once again it was a small volume, easily hidden away. And here we see rays of Tyndale's scholarly joy; of Deuteronomy, the last of the five books, he writes, 'this is a book worthy to be read in day and night and never to be out of hands . . . it is easy and light and a very pure gospel'.

Moreover, just as he did in the New Testament, Tyndale found phrases from the Hebrew (in the New Testament it was from the Greek and Latin) which seemed to have been in the air immemorially. That was one of his gifts. He coined new phrases from old. He had a spectacular talent for making the ordinary poetic and unforgettable. 'Am I my brother's keeper?', 'men of renown', 'every man's hand against him', 'the fat of the land', 'let there be light' – just a handful of examples from Genesis. Tyndale seems to have fallen in love with Hebrew. 'The proportion of the Hebrew tongue agreeth a thousand times more with the English than with the Latin,' he wrote.

It is still a mystery where Tyndale learned his Hebrew. It was not taught in Oxford in Tyndale's time there. In this, 'Europe', as often, was ahead. A polyglot Bible came out in Madrid between 1514 and 1517, putting Latin, Greek and Hebrew texts side by side. In 1506, the German scholar Reuchlin printed a Hebrew grammar for students, and was condemned by the Pope. Luther's Pentateuch from the Hebrew was published in 1534 but he had been working on it with other scholars for some years and Tyndale could have secured and tapped into that on visits to Wittenberg. Luther is certainly a source. But Tyndale uses rather than quotes him. Like all other books, those of Luther are there to be of service. Whatever the route, Tyndale found his way to Hebrew, got hold of a grammar and mastered it. And the monosyllables bed the work. 'And he ate and drank and rose up and went his way,' from Genesis; 'and he took a stone of the place . . . and laid him down in the same place to sleep . . .'

To master Hebrew, to see the Pentateuch through the printers and shipped to England, to root, yet again, imperishable phrases, sentences and rhythms into the English language, and to do so in conditions of constant harassment and danger, was surely a mighty task. What he did with these five books alone has outlasted most of the achievements of his age.

But there was one more inescapable challenge: to return to his passion, the Scriptures, the New Testament, and improve it to the extent that it was to become the source of speech and written English throughout the world.

* * *

The historian and Tyndale scholar David Daniell has called Tyndale's 1534 Revised New Testament 'the glory of his life's work'. Like a multitude of others, I agree with him.

Tyndale's prologue begins: 'Here thou hast (most dear reader) the New Testament or covenant made with us of God in Christ's blood.'

Tyndale's name appears on the title page of this translation – for the first time. This is to distinguish it from the versions that were being plagiarized – sometimes by his former assistants. Printed in Antwerp, it is a book of 400 pages which, like its predecessor, can be held in the hand and hidden quite easily. This time there are prologues to all the books and wood-cut prints in Revelation. There are further notes and notices – a table of set readings from the Gospels – at the back.

His disclaimers are in the first prologue. He says that this is a version 'which I have looked over again . . . with all diligence and compared it with the Greek, and have weeded out its many faults, which lack of help at the beginning and oversight did sow therein'. His Greek had improved and Hebrew had entered his vocabulary. He writes, 'If ought seems changed, or not altogether agreeing with the Greek, let the finder of the fault consider the Hebrew phrase or manner of speech left in the Greek words.' He then gives grammatical examples to clarify his methods. He also promises to work further on this book if faults are brought to his attention. He is setting out a lifetime's work in progress. Had he been spared . . .

Scholars tell us that this version begins to move away from 'hard-Lutheran' to a more English radical reformism which surely pervades the character of the book. It is another reason, I think, that although this 1534 edition draws from the Greek, the Latin and the Hebrew, it is an essential distillation of the best that English could then offer with the addition of Tyndale's genius for invention.

There were many fine-tunings of the 1526 version, of which these are a few: 'O ye endowed with little faith' has become 'O ye of little faith' – from a good sense to perfection; 'there is no Prophet without honour' becomes 'a Prophet is not without honour'. He made over 5,000 such revisions.

The King James Authorized Version of 1611 was to leave most of this untouched. The 1534 New Testament still stands as a magnificent masterpiece to be compared in influence only to Shakespeare, who took much from

Tyndale without knowing it. The English language was exceptional in having two geniuses at its source: one of the imagination, the other of translation. One made the mind soar, the other earthed it for 500 years more.

8

Betrayal and execution

In the early 1530s conditions seemed to be improving for Protestantism in England to the extent that an accommodation with Protestants became possible – an end to treating them as the enemy. Anne Boleyn's pregnancy tripped Henry's next move. He could not tolerate an illegitimate child, nor would his kingdom. In 1533 he wrenched an annulment from the Pope, declared his marriage to Katherine null and void, turned his back on European Catholicism and married Anne Boleyn. Through her and with some support from Cromwell, Tyndale's translation looked hopeful of victory.

As proof of this, it seemed, Sir Thomas More was arrested for treason. He had failed to swear an oath affirming the legitimacy of Anne and Henry's marriage. He refused to deny the supremacy of the Pope.

His sentence was to be hanged but cut down while he was still alive, castrated, his entrails cut out and burned before his eyes, and then beheaded. The King showed mercy. He was merely beheaded, on 6 July 1535. His severed head was boiled until it was black and displayed on London Bridge.

* * *

In 1535 Tyndale was living with a friend, Thomas Poyntz, and his wife at the English House in Antwerp. While he was there, one of his assistants, Miles Coverdale, was working on an English version of the Bible, requested by the King (to whom it would be dedicated), unashamedly and in quantity mostly lifted from his master, William Tyndale. It is unlikely that Tyndale would not have had word of this, yet no mention of it is made by him or those around him. Perhaps Coverdale chose or was forced to be discreet.

No truce had been declared. It must have seemed cruel that at last an English Bible was being prepared, massively dependent on Tyndale's work, and he still an outlaw and uncredited.

Nor was Tyndale unaware that at the court of the Emperor Charles in Brussels resentment continued unabated towards Henry VIII for abandoning Katherine, the aunt of the Emperor, and a rallying point in Catholic Europe. Charles's spies were still out searching for English Protestants. Tyndale was a prime target. Yet the English House was a strong retreat, bringing wealth to Antwerp. And besides, who could identify Tyndale? He had escaped capture for almost a decade now.

It was someone from Oxford, Tyndale's old university, and his old home territory, the West Country, who fingered him. Henry Phillips had robbed his rich father by gambling money given him to take to someone in London, and from then on he spiralled deeply into disgrace, lies, cheating and eventually treachery. He hated Henry VIII and all Lutherans and privately declared himself to be a fanatical Catholic. To Tyndale he posed as a Protestant.

After a period of desperation, Phillips managed to convince the procurer general at the Emperor's court that he could spy out three of the most prominent English Lutherans in Antwerp. One of these was Tyndale. It is likely that the procurer general, the Emperor's attorney, advanced substantial expenses.

Phillips, using the Oxford connection, eventually winkled an introduction to Tyndale in the English House and into the house of Thomas Poyntz. Poyntz took a dislike to him and mistrusted him, but Tyndale warmed to this ingratiating young Englishman bringing news from abroad. We know that Tyndale sorely missed his country, his language and his friends and perhaps Phillips might have allayed the pangs of homesickness. Or it could be that Tyndale had grown careless from the stretch of security he had enjoyed in Antwerp.

Fatally for Tyndale, Phillips called on him while Poyntz was away. Phillips wanted to take him to dinner but Tyndale insisted that Phillips accompany him to a dinner with friends. Either way, Phillips had set his trap.

Outside Poyntz's house there was a long entry, a narrow alley which made it difficult for two to walk side by side. Phillips insisted that Tyndale, who was a slightly built man of no great height, go ahead of him. As they came towards the exit of this alley, officers of the Emperor were waiting for them, and the taller Phillips pointed his finger at Tyndale. The officers said that they 'pitied his simplicity' when they took him. Tyndale is said to have then dined with the procurer general, while his few possessions – chiefly books – were cleared from his room and taken away. This suggests a respect and a courtesy which at that stage must have made the arrest seem less threatening. After dinner Tyndale was escorted to Vilvoorde Castle, built in 1374, 18 miles from Antwerp, about six miles from Brussels. He was there for 16 months.

* * *

When I first thought through the previous passage about Phillips, I had planned to make it longer, more suspenseful, more detailed. I had considered how Phillips had so completely won over Tyndale's confidence – at one point Tyndale lent him 40 shillings. Was it just because of the Oxford connection, or did Phillips also bring back fond memories of the interests of the West Country? His father was three times an MP, sheriff of the county, perhaps acquainted with Tyndale's family and friends in the area. We know from what Tyndale told Stephen Vaughan that he was lonely for friends and home. And then there was this compound of innocence and fearlessness in Tyndale. The one would have asked no probing questions about a well-bred, Oxford-educated fellow Englishman; the other would have taken no precautions, despite the concern of his good friend Thomas Poyntz.

There would have been much in Phillips's character and actions to be angry, even vicious about, but I lost heart. That this transcendent scholar at the peak of his power should have been cut off by such an inconsequential petty thief and liar, that he was netted at last by such a nasty little piece of work is so disproportionate. And imagine what Tyndale could have done with a few more years. Finished translating the Old Testament, including the Psalms – with all the languages he now controlled, they could have become a pinnacle of English poetry. He would have gone back to the New Testament and made what is so fine even better. More essays, more sermons. And Protestant England might forgive and welcome the man who was to give it voice . . . he could have lived a warmer, freer life, been with old friends, been celebrated and known for the best reasons. Instead of which we have the Judas finger of this perfidious and despicable man, which pointed him to his death.

* * *

Efforts to release Tyndale began immediately. The English merchants in Antwerp wrote to Brussels complaining that their corporate and diplomatic privilege had been abused. Their anger was public and Phillips was reported to be 'marvellously afraid'.

There were letters to England but the English powers were strapped. How could Henry – now excommunicated – appeal to the Holy Roman Emperor for clemency for a Lutheran Englishman, especially after ditching the Emperor's close relation, the now ex-Queen Katherine? As for Cromwell – he seems to have tried but not been able to pursue the case, especially as time dragged on with the inevitable dilution of interest, and there were bigger concerns in London. Managing the unpredictable Henry, who was casting a covetous eye on the wealthy and resplendent monasteries of England, was a full-time occupation. And besides, Henry, it seemed, was a Protestant under Protest. He never ceased to hanker for Catholicism – but a Catholicism on his own terms which the Church of Rome could not and dared not allow. So the Defender of the Faith became the Enemy of the Faith and England was cut loose.

One man who acted in a most courageous manner was Thomas Poyntz. Perhaps he blamed himself for not affording better security to Tyndale. But it seems to me that he acted out of honour and friendship. Although it was to prove disastrous for his own fortune and a near thing for his life, he sailed into battle.

He wrote to his elder brother in England, who had some influence at court. He said that the King had sent letters (written by Cromwell) to the court in Brussels in favour of Tyndale. These, Poyntz claimed, had been blocked. Poyntz adds, 'this poor man, William Tyndale, hath lain in my house three quarters of a year. The King has never a truer hearted subject to his Grace this day living.'

Poyntz seemed to be getting somewhere, especially as these letters from Cromwell – although elusive – were apparently known about and could, just, have become a bargaining chip. Phillips got wind of this, and blackened Poyntz's name; he successfully encouraged the procurer general to detain Poyntz and put him under house arrest in Brussels. The procurer general built up a case against him, and interrogations, at which Phillips was always present, went on from the beginning of November until the end of January. He was also to accompany the procurer general's inquisitors when they went to interrogate Tyndale in prison. Phillips was constantly afraid that something might be said to undermine him and took no chances. The disturbing and rather puzzling mystery is why he was allowed such access and his word taken as the gold standard for all evidence regarding Tyndale. Tyndale's eventual execution, of course, would secure his final pay-off.

Poyntz realized that once the questioning was done, he would be imprisoned with little chance of release. He escaped, evaded his pursuers, and got to England. He was banished from the Netherlands, his wife refused to join him in England, his business was ruined. In 1547 he succeeded to his family's ancestral manor in North Ockenden but it was said he was too poor to live there.

In Antwerp as in London it was dangerous to be known as a friend of a man thought by many to be a threat to the peace of Tudor England. Yet there were those who stood by Tyndale. Stephen Vaughan seems to have held on to hope for him, and even in April 1536 – after Tyndale had been in prison for about a year – Vaughan wrote, from the Netherlands, to Cromwell: 'If now you send me but your letter to the Privy Council, I could deliver Tyndale from the fire, so it come by time for else it would be too late.'

There was no reply. Tyndale stayed in prison.

Had he returned to England he would almost certainly have been burned at the stake. He had too many enemies, and heresy was a crime for all seasons. Of Tyndale it was said that 'he could not hedge, nor trim, nor speak with a double voice,' and in Stokesley there was a burning Bishop of London, who saw him as an out-and-out traitor to the King and the faith.

Tyndale was left to his fate. His imprisonment dragged on. His reputation was too high to threaten but too great to ignore. Time, it was hoped by his persecutors, would wear him down. Meanwhile let him stay dungeoned.

* * *

In August 1536, after more than a year and a quarter in prison, having been officially condemned as a heretic, Tyndale was degraded from the priesthood.

This 'degrading' was a formal, humiliating and public event. Tyndale was taken out of prison in his priestly clothes and escorted to a platform on which were seated a corps of dignitaries, including bishops. It is reported that a big and fashionable crowd assembled, hoping to see both the degradation and an execution. It is conceivable that there was some silent support. He was a rare specimen. Anointing oil was symbolically scraped from his hands, the bread and chalice of wine from the Mass were handed to him and then taken from him. His ceremonial vestments were removed from him. He was now no longer a priest. William Tyndale was a man of consequence and influence and this was a terrible humiliation. The injustice must have been very hard to bear – but there is no complaint reported from Tyndale.

Once the ceremony was completed – it scarcely needs to be said that no ceremony of this kind appears in the pages of the Scriptures – Tyndale was handed over to the secular authorities and taken back to his cell. The crowd was cheated of its death – for a while. The authorities were still nervous.

He went back into the control of the procurer general, whose fee for the capturing and executing of Tyndale, added to the cut he got from the sale of Tyndale's books and effects (which would support his expenses in prison), was far and away the biggest he had ever received. He had his own reasons to drag it out.

The procurer general had organized 17 commissioners – theologians, lawyers, members of the Privy Council – to question Tyndale in his cell, following his arrest, with Phillips always at the door. Tyndale continued writing and studying while imprisoned and produced what would become a book, *Faith Alone Justifies Before God*. We have not a scrap of evidence that he doubted God in any way during this ordeal.

We do, however, have a letter in which he describes his condition. The ancient Vilvoorde Castle, in which Tyndale was incarcerated, was to be abandoned post-Tyndale, and a later prison built on the spot. Its replacement was not as sunk down and dungeoned as the original, but I found it a bleak and cold place and the cells are oppressive: it is easy to imagine Tyndale locked in there.

Tyndale's letter was written in September 1535. It was addressed to someone in authority, thought to be the Marquis of Bergen-op-Zoom, the Privy Councillor to whom Cromwell wrote. The Marquis was also the governor of Vilvoorde Castle.

> I believe, right worshipful, that you are not unaware of what may have been determined concerning me. Wherefore I beg your lordship and by the Lord Jesus, that if I am to remain here through the winter, you will request the commissary to have the kindness to send me, from the goods of mine that he hath, a warmer cap; for I suffer greatly from cold in the head, and am afflicted by a perpetual catarrh, which is much increased in this cell; a warmer coat, also, for this which I have is very thin, a piece of cloth too to patch my leggings. My overcoat is worn out; my shirts are also worn out. He has a woollen shirt if he will be good enough to send it. I have also with him leggings of thicker cloth to put on above; he also has warmer night-caps.
>
> And I ask to be allowed to have a lamp in the evening; it is indeed wearisome sitting alone in the dark.
>
> But most of all I beg and beseech your clemency to be urgent with the commissary that he will kindly permit me to have the Hebrew bible, Hebrew Grammar and Hebrew Dictionary, that I may pass the time in that study. In return may you obtain what you most desire, so only that it be for the salvation of your soul. But if any other decision has been taking concerning me, to be carried out before winter, I will be patient, abiding the will of God, to the glory of the grace of my Lord Jesus Christ, Whose spirit (I pray) may ever direct your heart. Amen. W. Tindalus.

We have no evidence of a reply.

* * *

The 17 inquisitors had taken it in turns to hammer away at him over many months, questioning, quoting and, one assumes (from previous evidence), misquoting him, determined that the admission of heresy would come out of his own mouth. We have records of some of Tyndale's rigorous and erudite replies and it is fair to assume that on matters to do with the Scriptures and the Old Testament he was more than a match for all of them. We are told that he asked for English divines to interrogate him, as he wanted to hear his own language even if it expressed opposition.

The foregone conclusion was delivered in April 1536. The punishment was that he would be degraded (which took place at the ceremony in August described above) and then burned at the stake.

Foxe, who wrote so warmly about Tyndale and whose praise, which once seemed excessive but from later scholarship now seems accurate, continued in that vein to the end. He reveals that Tyndale converted the keeper and others of his household, and that all those in the Castle who got to know Tyndale 'reported of him, that if he were not a good Christian man, they could not tell whom to trust'.

When Tyndale walked through the crowded streets to the place of execution in the small town of Vilvoorde on 6 October 1536, his words had already been shamelessly plagiarized by Miles Coverdale, his former assistant and friend. An authorized Bible in English had been published with the blessing of Henry VIII. Tyndale would have prayed but could not have known that Protestantism would take wing on his words and fly over England and from there around the globe. He would be ignorant and most likely indifferent to the centuries of literary praise which would

Part 2

THE LEGACY

9

The Bible of Shakespeare

Tyndale's wider influence – which can be called immeasurable – was founded on the King James Version of 1611. Luther had been and would rightly forever be seen, in terms of the rupture in European thought and politics, as the key man in the Reformation. Tyndale learned much from him by example and from his works. However, it was the English and not the German language which circled the planet. At the end of Elizabeth's reign, the words 'the British Empire' came into play and that nudging boast quite soon and unexpectedly billowed into an empire 'on which the sun never set'. It was and remains a giddy, disruptive, at once both proud and damaging, almost freakish, conquest for the English, or more correctly the British.

The way in which its language was taken around the globe by buccaneering and trading ships, the missions and explorations of the British, spread it to an extent never before achieved. It became the first language of Australia, New Zealand and Canada, the second language of India, South Africa, the West Indies, and was soon pecking its way into the word hoard worldwide.

Then came the United States of America. The English who went to America to find a New England far from the oppression and corruption of their homeland were, largely, a people of the book: Presbyterians and Dissenters of several denominations, and some Anglicans. It is not an exaggeration to say that in the early years of that defining first and second phase of settlement on the East Coast, it was the Bible which bonded, characterized and sustained them. And so when the extraordinary power of America accelerated to cultural and economic domination, it was again on the wings of the English language that it flew over oceans and continents. And that English was founded in the King James Bible, still to this day the solemn, even sacred, book on which American Presidents swear their oath of office.

The King James Bible New Testament is almost entirely Tyndale's work – now estimated at more than 93 per cent. In the Old Testament, the books he had translated (the first five) are about 85 per cent Tyndale. His voice rises from his ashes and we hear it everywhere – in international diplomacy, on 'world' committees of multiple purposes, new English-based dialects and new versions of the Bible. Tyndale's work is the fundamental engine, the touchstone and the driving force through its influence on literature, films, theatre, television and radio and education. It is expressed through the King James Bible of 1611.

The Coverdale Bible was published in 1535 – Coverdale did some work on those parts of the Old Testament that Tyndale had not reached and tweaked a little, even provided new sentences. But it was Tyndale's. In 1537, the far more Tyndale-based Matthew Bible was published, licensed by the King.

Thomas Matthew was the politic pen name of John Rogers, good friend and colleague of Tyndale. He was faithful to his friend. He put the initials W.T. at the end of the Prophets. Most of all, he honoured Tyndale's work in this 1537 edition, which itself became the source for other 'versions' which appeared throughout the century. When

Protestantism secured its grip – after the Catholic revenge of Queen Mary – more scholars turned their hand to what could prove a good earner. Tyndale's name, despite John Rogers's open tribute, was gradually eroded from public memory. Authorship was too profitable to share with a dead man. King Henry VIII, we are told, could not bear to hear his name spoken, so it did not help plagiarists to reveal their source. He was ghosted away, as anonymous as he had been for those pre-Phillips days in Antwerp.

But John Rogers did him the best of all favours. He was loyal to the original. He had helped Tyndale in his translation at the English House. When Tyndale was arrested, it is credibly reported that Rogers took Tyndale's translated manuscripts and his notes for further work, and went possibly to Wittenberg in order to prepare a fuller version. It has been observed that Rogers's translation of some books in the Old Testament bears a linguistic connection with the first five books finished by Tyndale – very unlike Coverdale's attempts. Perhaps Rogers had access to Tyndale's notes; perhaps a close scholarly bond with Tyndale at a fertile period enabled him to adopt and even imitate something of his master's style and learning. It is, again, helpful to quote from David Daniell of the Matthew Bible:

> What he did do triumphantly, was transmit the 200,000 words of Tyndale's Pentateuch and the even longer New Testament to a more influential English readership, and guarantee that Tyndale was the maker of most of the English bible for centuries to come. The three hundred odd changes that Rogers made dwindle into insignificance.

There are reports of congregations, after a church service, crowding around a local elder who read this Bible aloud to them. It was lapped up, the milk and honey they had been denied. Among the crowd, it is to be hoped, were ploughboys.

When I published a book on the impact of the King James Bible, 1611–2011, I mentioned how influential it had been on Shakespeare, among others. One reviewer pointed out that the King James Bible was published in 1611, and as Shakespeare died in 1615, having surrendered his quill a few years before that, then such a connection was impossible.

He was wrong. The Matthew Bible took Tyndale through the sixteenth century under almost perfect cover. After his marriage to Anne, Henry commanded that there be a Bible in English in every church in the land. It would also be read in schools, like the grammar school in Stratford-upon-Avon, and most likely in the houses of persons of substance, like Shakespeare's father. In short, I would claim that Shakespeare would have heard Tyndale day in, day out throughout his boyhood and adolescence. As we will see, his borrowings from Tyndale were numerous and fundamental, via the Matthew or the Great Bible.

What was true for Shakespeare was true for tens of thousands of others. Tyndale's influence began in 1526, increased in 1534 and continued 'under cover' until 1611. Since then it has been proved to be the unacknowledged legislator of the words so long and falsely ascribed to the scholars of King James.

It could be claimed that the unprecedented beauty of English verse in the theatre and in books of poetry, and of English prose in the Elizabethan age, would be moulded by Tyndale's sentences coupled with grammatical rules laid down by Erasmus.

The King James Bible has, since its publication, sold more copies than any other book in the world. After centuries of ignorance or wilful repression, we can no longer deny the overwhelming nature of Tyndale's contribution.

And above all, I think, his words – so clear, so open, so brilliantly and so deceptively common, commonplace – gave to the people of English the liberty to think rather than the duty to believe.

* * *

And so we arrive at the making of the King James Bible, the King James Version as it is known in the United States of America.

King James, who followed Elizabeth to the throne in 1603, was a serious Bible scholar. He prided himself on his knowledge and on his ability to translate the Bible from one language into another. The King James Bible came about partly because he wanted to show off his knowledge to the scholars and churchmen, and to his new and, to James, fabulously rich kingdom of England, and partly to unite his realm. The Protestant revolution had soon bred splinter groups of varying Presbyterian intensities of faith in Scotland and England. The Anglican Church seemed, to these Dissenters, to have held on to far too many popish characteristics.

James proposed to dazzle them all with his erudition – which he did, and with speeches of inordinate length at a conference at Hampton Court. After the performance, at the request of a Presbyterian, he cleverly commissioned a new Bible. This aimed to unite all the factions into one Church under him – James. *His* Bible. King James more prominent than God. No dissenting marginal comments, which could be treasonous – comparing kings to tyrants, for example; no drifting away from the purity of the words; the whole authorized by James himself, who would, if he requested it, have the right to read and correct it before publication. Agreed? Agreed.

About 50 scholars were employed. England at that time was waist deep in biblical scholarship. In what other subject could men of high intellect find a place to shine? Science was marginal or taboo. The law was important but hardly as glamorous or as important as the affairs of God, Christ and eternal life. The two universities taught classics and theology which could lead to fat livings, preferment and good reputation. James's scholars were a formidable company.

In the event, following the pattern of this period in English history which was active in forming companies, there were four companies. Between them the Bible was quartered. They took it seriously and there were regular readings and checkings.

In his preface to the Bible, Miles Smyth wrote:

> Translation it is that openeth the window to let in the light: that breaketh the shell that we may eat the kernel; that putteth aside the kernel that we may look into the most holy place, that removeth the cover of the well that we may come by the water, even as Jacob rolled away the stone from the mouth of the well.

Fine words. But they buttered no parsnips. It is all but inexplicable that these men of substance in studies key to the project spent several dedicated years examining all the Bibles in English from Coverdale in 1535, yet failed to recognize that Tyndale was again and again the key author. As already said, the most recent close textual research has proved that more than 93 per cent of the New Testament in the King James Bible is from the hand of William Tyndale! And that more than 85 per cent of the five key books of the Old Testament are also by Tyndale!

By accident and design, his name and contribution had been erased. Perhaps his name was still too toxic, almost a century on. Perhaps it was down to ignorance and the fact that his versions were unattributed.

The world was misled for centuries. This is Tyndale's Bible. It is dressed up fit for the conceit of a King in the full plumage of his new inheritance; the 50 scholars have received inordinate praise over the centuries and 'proved' that 'a committee' can write an imperishable work. (Who needs an individual? Hollywood producers have loved employing gangs of writers using King James as their precedent.) And it's all rot. Tyndale did it, or far and away the bulk of it. Mostly alone; always the author.

Yet even up to the twentieth century and in the hands of one of that century's deservedly finest poets – T. S. Eliot – Tyndale is slighted. Scholars – distinguished, some of them from a social class above Tyndale and basking in a privileged establishment status which Eliot admired and Tyndale never achieved – were still given the upper hand. Even when they made a poor fist of it.

For instance, writing in *The Athenaeum* in May 1919, Eliot examines Tyndale's opening lines of Genesis:

> In the beginning God created heaven and earth. The world was void and empty; and darkness was upon the deep and the spirit of God moved upon the water.

Yet he prefers the King James Version – from Dean Lancelot Andrewes, a favourite of T. S. Eliot's:

> In the beginning God created the heaven and the earth. And the earth was without form, and void; and darkness was upon the face of the deep. And the spirit of God moved upon the face of the waters.

Thirty-nine words compared to Tyndale's 29. The key words 'deep', 'void' and 'darkness' are Tyndale's. Tyndale says it all but more punchily, more simply. This, I think, reveals a fashion that has grown up since Tyndale's death. The Protestant establishment, having lost Latin as their book of authority, introduced elaboration wherever they could. Was this to claim back authority from what they might have seen as the over-common, over-dangerous Tyndale? They reintroduced elite cosiness and wherever possible tried to smooth the edge of Tyndale's translation.

Thankfully – if we can assume that most if not all of the 50 were ignorant of Tyndale's thread through all the translations they studied – they do not seem to have picked that up. He was a shadow. Had they known, I think they may well have settled down to carve him out. Their ignorance was a blessing.

So we have Tyndale. His scholarship amassed for the faith reached many countries and founded a modern English as an indirect consequence. There are long passages of Tyndale we can read today as easily as we can read contemporary work. Chaucer – although wonderful – has to be studied and translated. The Elizabethans, based on Tyndale's work, still soar; as do later generations for whom Tyndale stands firm, clear and speaking to us in what he made our common tongue.

His words, idioms and phrases are still spoken daily and this continued use proves not only their quality but their indispensability. Tyndale sought this unceasingly in the deepest reaches of the rarely tapped reservoir of ordinariness. From this flood words which give us meaning.

I have quoted a few along the way. Here are a few more, from the Tyndale Bible published in 1611 under the cover of King James. His – own – words – still.

'See the writing on the wall', 'cast the first stone', 'the salt of the earth', 'a thorn in the flesh', 'fight the good fight', 'from strength to strength', 'the blind lead the blind', 'sick unto death', 'broken-hearted', 'clear-eyed', 'the powers that be'. Beautiful . . . and not to forget the Lord's Prayer, the Beatitudes and the powerfully lasting rhythms in the prose of the Gospels. On they go and it seems will go on. Like Shakespeare, these words, these and more phrases, are an x-ray of who we are. 'And the word was made flesh and dwelt among us.' And dwells among us still.

10

A force for good

The primary influence of the King James Bible was on its congregations of readers and listeners. It was the message and the messenger of the rise and expansion of Protestantism. Religion took English around the world. Faith made it a language to be treasured. The Bible was a practical resource, furnishing a vocabulary, a set of moral precepts and ammunition for a multitude of arguments.

As has been pointed out, it was the global influence of first Great Britain and then the USA which took the language on its travels. The Bible was instrumental and almost accidental in that process. Whichever way you describe it – and it could be half a dozen of one and six of the other – the Bible spoke English to much of the world and became the second language in those in which it did not occupy first place.

Would any Bible have done? Possibly. Would a non-Tyndale Bible have had the same effect? Probably not. Tyndale's words penetrated hearts in profound ways. It spoke to feelings as well as minds. Is there any way of calculating the difference there might have been between Tyndale and non-Tyndale? Highly unlikely: for as we see, there were layers on layers in Tyndale. It made him meat for the development of democracy, for instance, to take just one example which was not there in the Vulgate. Nor was it deeply implanted in Wycliffe. Tyndale's Bible taught more than the working of God and the words of Jesus; it set out the foundational conditions for a new, much more egalitarian society.

* * *

The Bible as translated largely by Tyndale is itself a work of the highest literary achievement and this has been recognized and acclaimed by writers, commentators and readers. Enough has been quoted in this book to confirm that it possesses beauty, memorability and also a force that has driven its influence through centuries of echoes, references, imitations and praise. It is literature on the page and on the tongue, through the eyes and through the ears; this remarkable dual effect smacks as much of the playwright as of the scholar. But Tyndale had an apprenticeship in drama – his open-air sermons, tempered doubtlessly by the responses of his meeting – and this together with his conviction that everyone, high and low, learned and illiterate, had to share in these words and messages, gave him this exceptional genius. He honoured and privileged the monosyllable.

He has been coupled with Shakespeare in his influence on the language. In terms of idioms and new words, they are neck and neck. But Tyndale came first and it was he who – largely through Hebrew – introduced forms of sentences which slotted perfectly into dramatic verse (and later prose – viz D. H. Lawrence). Shakespeare quotes from the Bible about 1,350 times. These quotations are from the Bibles he heard and read – the Great Bible, the Matthew Bible and probably the Geneva Bible – all of which were Tyndale in disguise. Tyndale came to Shakespeare with no name: but Shakespeare recognized him and did what so many writers do – seized on what he needed. Apart from anything else, the Bible was a treasure vault of stories. Shakespeare was an expert plunderer.

The historian A. L. Rowse points out that there are definite allusions to 42 books of the Bible. Cain is referred to 25 times, Samson seven, David six, Solomon nine, the Whore of Babylon seven . . .

And there are specific stealings. Here are some of them.

Are not two sparrows sold for a farthing? And one of them shall not fall on the ground without your Father.

(Matthew 10.29)

There's a special providence in the fall of a sparrow. If it be now, 'tis not to come: if it be not to come, it will be now.

(*Hamlet*)

Eye hath not seen, nor ear heard, neither have entered into the heart of man, the things which God hath prepared for them that love him. (1 Corinthians 2.9)

The eye of man hath not heard, the ear of man hath not seen, man's hand is not able to taste, what my dream may mean!

(*A Midsummer Night's Dream* – and the sweetest teasing tribute to Tyndale that he could have hoped for)

For with what judgement ye judge, ye shall be judged: and with what measure ye mete, it shall be measured to you again. (Matthew 7.2)

Death for Death. Haste still pays Haste and leisure answers leisure; like doth quit like, and Measure still for Measure.

(*Measure for Measure*)

It is difficult fully to appreciate so much of the best

of literature in English since the time of Shakespeare without a thorough knowledge of the King James/Tyndale Bible.

* * *

For where Shakespeare led, a train of writers have followed. John Donne, for example, wrote, 'there are not so eloquent books in the world as the Scriptures. The style of the Scriptures is a diligent and artificial style and a great part of it is as musical, is as metrical, is a measured composition in verse.' (This chimes in well with Shelley's dismissal of any essential difference between prose and verse.)

Writers lift themes and stories from the Bible – Milton above all, with *Paradise Lost, Paradise Regained* and *Samson Agonistes* especially (for me, the truest to Tyndale's style and rhythms); and John Bunyan's *Pilgrim's Progress* which in one period challenged the Bible in popularity. '*Pilgrim's Progress* seems to be a complete reflection of Scripture,' wrote Matthew Arnold. Bunyan's prose is a parallel version of Tyndale's. Another lower-class writer, Daniel Defoe, is steeped in Tyndale. Brought up as a Dissenter, at one stage set on being a Presbyterian minister, his books, especially *Moll Flanders* and *Robinson Crusoe*, draw on a repertoire of direct quotation.

On it goes. Jonathan Swift, devout clergyman, in *A Letter to a Young Gentleman* describes how seriously a sermon should be undertaken. William Blake seems to be in constant conversation with the Bible. Even when Christianity is transformed into pantheism, as in Wordsworth, or dismissed with sweeping exuberance by Byron, it is there. Testaments Old and New are under the skin of so many writers of the day – the Brontës, Mrs Gaskell, Tennyson and, perhaps more than any other, Charles Dickens. There is a passage in *Bleak House* often mocked for its sentimentality but to anyone of sympathetic sensibility it is a masterful demonstration of the Bible's capacity to offer hope in the worst of times.

Little Jo, the ten-year-old crossing sweeper, is described by Dickens in a searing paragraph as he trails the streets behind Allan Woodcourt, a Christian doctor whom he senses might save him. Jo is an outcast – like so many children we see today in refugee camps, in flight, hungry, dying. And, in Dickens's day, as in ours, the world had much sympathy for 'foreign grown savages' but less for the home-made article. Dickens describes Jo as he knows others see him:

> dirty, ugly, disagreeable to all senses, in body a common creature of the common streets, only a soul in heaven. Homely filth begrimes him, homely parasites devour him, homely sores are in him, homely rags are on him; native ignorance, the growth of English soil and climate, sinks his moral nature lower than the beasts that perish. Stand forth, Jo, in uncompromising colours! From the sole of thy foot to the crown of thy head, there is nothing interesting about thee.

Then we witness Dickens's belief in Christianity and his use of Tyndale.

Allan Woodcourt, sympathetic to the boy, is at Jo's bedside. Jo is dying – undernourished and starved of everything that makes a boy human: yet the boy has hope. Woodcourt reassures him that he will be buried in a churchyard next to someone, as the boy says,

> 'as was wery good to me, wery good to me indeed he was . . . He used to say "I am as poor as you today, Jo," he ses. I wants

to tell him I am as poor as him now, and have come there to be laid along with him . . . will you promise to have me took there, sir?'

'I will indeed.'

'Thank ee, sir . . . thank ee . . . it's turned very dark, sir. Is there any light a-coming?'

'It is coming fast, Jo.'

'I hear you, sir, in the dark but I'm a-gropin', a-gropin' – let me catch hold of your hand.'

'Jo, can you say what I say?'

'I'll say anythink as you say, sir, for I know it's good.'

'OUR FATHER.'

'Our Father . . . yes, that's very good, sir.'

'WHICH ART IN HEAVEN.'

'Art in Heaven – is the light a-comin', sir?'

'It is close at hand. HALLOWED BE THY NAME.'

'Hallowed – be – thy – '

The light is come upon the dark benighted way. Dead!

Dead, your Majesty. Dead, my lords and gentlemen. Dead, Right Reverends and Worthy Reverends of every order. Dead, men and women born with Heavenly compassion in your hearts. And dying thus around us every day.

* * *

For Dickens, like Tyndale, a Christian belief fed by the words of the Bible could translate into hope even at the last and lowest moments. Those who mock this passage's sentimentality fail to understand its truth both to the times that were and to the conditions that remain. Its sense of the best in life, the soul of it, as once would have been said, remain. Religions change their name and form and fall away. But what Dickens and others – writers or not – took from the

Bible was an essential, pure caring one for the other. That remains. So too the creeds and epistles, the parables and stories which so clearly inspired writers – beyond Dickens and beyond England – Harriet Beecher Stowe, Nathaniel Hawthorne, Melville, Faulkner, T. S. Eliot, Baldwin, Steinbeck, Toni Morrison.

As long as and wherever the King James/Tyndale Bible is accepted, taught and believed as part of the culture, it has had and will have influence for good as well as, on the other hand, providing a vocabulary for authoritarianism.

The Wesleyans took the Bible into the plantations in the south of North America. Their vigorous and rousing methods of preaching from the Bible and of singing hymns made from verses in the Bible were key factors, allied to the influence of African chants and spiritualism, which led to 'church music' – choral singing, clapping, rhythmic praise for the Lord, then to 'soul music', to the blues, to jazz, to rock'n'roll, and to the layerings of popular music, which is a unique contribution to world culture. The Bible could seize the imagination and alchemize it into action.

And this went on across society. Evangelists became philanthropists. Women made their earliest political entry into society through the work of healing and helping. They did this in the poorest, saddest districts, inspired by the words they read in the Bible. The Bible became their sword and shield. Perhaps, again, we have to say that 'any Bible would have done' – but – for words for those songs?

Women seized on the Bible mainly because of its messages and its concern with care for the poor and dispossessed and its compassion, so well expressed by Dickens. But it was also because in a Christian society it enabled them to take part in social and political life in a way largely denied all except the few who in previous ages whispered advice in royal anterooms. The women's movement, it could be argued, has one of its fundamental pillars in the Bible.

A few examples would include Mary Astell, a High Church Anglican Tory who set out her own view of Christian feminism in attacking John Locke, whose philosophy of freedom, she asserted, excluded half the human race. Joanna Southcott, a Methodist from Devon, inspired a large-scale apocalyptic movement which retained female leadership despite many challenges from men.

In Victorian Britain and at a similar time in America there was a spectacular surge in the creation of charitable organizations, all Bible-led, many driven forward by women. Octavia Hill, for example (1838–1912), worked as a child in a toy workshop. She was running it by the age of 14. It was subsidized by the Christian Socialists who liberated Octavia Hill into an extraordinary life of social reform. She campaigned successfully for social housing and for open spaces to be made available to the poor. She encouraged Bible study and attendance at Sunday Schools, often the only schooling available to the poor.

Then there was Ellen Ranyard, founder of Bible Women. She deliberately hired working-class women to distribute, sell and teach from the Bible.

Catherine Booth, wife of William, the founder of the Salvation Army, became a leading figure in transforming the condition of sweatshops and achieved a great victory in getting yellow phosphorous banned from matchmaking factories. This had inflicted 'phossy jaw' (necrosis of the bone) on the ill-paid girls in the factories.

Other examples of female agency connected with the Bible include: Josephine Butler and her attack on white slave traffic; Jane Addams, one of the earliest in a long list of American women activists who taught from the Bible; and there was a rapid growth of Bible Women in America.

Again and again it was the Bible as a book of wisdom and example that was the best way for women to make an appearance, then a claim, then exact an influence on the larger shaping of society towards a more just, kinder place. Much good has grown up in Christian countries, much that has transformed itself into secular pillars of social justice. We owe much of that to the Tyndale/King James Bible and to the women who saw it as a path to justice, hope and eventually influence and power.

Christianity has also been accused of many things which are unforgivable: inquisitions, child abuse, exercising a tyranny of thought and subservience to what Tyndale would have characterized as 'the Pope' rather than 'God'. But much good has come of the Church and in the slow progress towards a hoped-for equality in quality of life, the Bible and those who found revolution in it have improved the world.

On so many levels: music, art, drama and even science ... without God there might have been no law of gravity. Newton wanted, even needed, a prime sole mover, a first and all-inclusive Beginning to the Universe. He said that God was gravity and vice versa. Social groups, community work, choirs, good company, charity. While there will always be a dark side, sometimes a walk on the bright side is instructive.

Finally, I think that democratic systems everywhere – particularly in Britain and America, still evolving – find their basis in Tyndale. He was the most profound democrat. All souls, all lives, were equally valuable. This was unthinkable on any large scale until those who read the 1611 version dug in and found their common North Star. Tyndale's immovable belief was that we are all equal in the sight of God and in the lives of other men and women; therefore God's words must be made plain.

We see it emerging in the pamphlets and speeches of the English Civil Wars. We see it develop in the dissenting movements which, barred from the universities and high offices, set up a state within the State of Britain and found in America a new state to build from its foundation. We see this religion-bound, democratic determination in the freedom movements in America, among women in country after country. It stems from the Bible, a book whose influence continues, seen and unseen, but at its best still at the heart of our civilization.

Postscript
Genius discarded?

Yet, in this country, the King James Bible has been allowed to fade away over the past few decades. While Shakespeare in all his Elizabethan and Jacobean pageant of language is played, filmed, televised and read more and more and in the original without dissent, it was decided that Tyndale was too complicated! This has proved to be a dreadful mistake. We have discarded a genius and are every day the poorer for it. I see it as no accident that Anglican congregations have fallen away since the King James Bible was abandoned.

The Anglican Church has more or less outlawed the King James Version. It pops up now and then but with far less regularity and authority than it deserves. Why not have Tyndale/King James services in every church and every school on the first week of every month? For non-Christians it would be a feast of language, adventure and argument. For all who listened it would be to hear and understand the deepest spring of our cultural history through the mind of a unique genius: William Tyndale.

Further reading

Melvyn Bragg, *The Adventure of English*, London: Hodder & Stoughton, 2003

Melvyn Bragg, *Twelve Books That Changed the World*, London: Hodder & Stoughton, 2006

Melvyn Bragg, *The Book of Books: The Radical Impact of the King James Bible, 1611–2011*, London: Hodder & Stoughton, 2011

David Daniell, *William Tyndale: A Biography*, New Haven, CT: Yale University Press, 1993

Charles Dickens, *Bleak House*, London: Penguin Classics, 2003

John Foxe, *Foxe's Book of Martyrs*, Oxford: Oxford University Press, 2009

Thomas More, *Utopia*, London: Penguin Classics, 1981

Thomas More, *Dialogue Concerning Heresies*, Strongsville, OH: Scepter, 2006

William Tyndale, *The Obedience of a Christian Man*, London: Penguin Classics, 2000

William Tyndale, *The Parable of the Wicked Mammon*, Oxford: Benediction Books, 2009

William Tyndale, *The Practice of Prelates*, CrossReach Publications, 2015

The Works of William Tyndale, two volumes, Banner of Truth Trust, East Peoria, IL: Versa Press, 2010

Index

Index

Index

Index

Index